100
GREATS

WALSALL
FOOTBALL CLUB

100 GREATS

WALSALL
FOOTBALL CLUB

WRITTEN BY
GEOFF ALLMAN

TEMPUS

Tempus Publishing Limited
The Mill, Brimscombe Port,
Stroud, Gloucestershire, GL5 2QG

ISBN 0 7524 2226 X

Typesetting and origination by
Tempus Publishing Limited
Printed in Great Britain by
Midway Colour Print, Wiltshire

Present and forthcoming titles from Tempus Publishing:

0 7524 2166 2	A False Stroke of Genius: The Wayne Larkins Story	John Wallace	£12.99
0 7524 2167 0	Lord's: Cathedral of Cricket (hb)	Stephen Green	£25.00
0 7524 2175 1	Leicestershire CCC: 100 Greats	Dennis Lambert	£12.00
0 7524 2180 8	Warwickshire CCC: 100 Greats	Robert Brooke	£12.00
0 7524 1834 3	Worcestershire County Cricket Club	Les Hatton	£9.99
0 7524 2194 8	Worcestershire CCC: 100 Greats	Les Hatton	£12.00
0 7524 2210 3	Homes of Speedway	Robert Bamford & John Jarvis	£17.99
0 7524 1862 9	Birmingham City FC: Images	Tony Matthews	£9.99
0 7524 2091 7	Walsall FC: Images	Geoff Allman	£9.99
0 7524 2056 9	West Brom FC: Images	Tony Matthews	£9.99
0 7524 2224 3	West Brom FC: 100 Greats	Tony Matthews	£12.00
0 7524 2217 0	The Ultimate Drop	George Rowland	£12.99
0 7524 1855 6	Football Programme	John Litster	£12.99
0 7524 2042 9	Forever England	Tony Williamson & Mark Shaoul	£17.99

This is the official biography of one of the greatest strikers to appear for Walsall. Lavishly illustrated with over 200 images, it follows Allan Clarke's career from the early days at Fellows Park, big money moves to Fulham and Leicester and the glory years with Leeds. It also looks at his games for England, his subsequent managerial career and his dream team. This is a fascinating read for anyone who remembers Sniffer's deadly finishing instinct.

Hardback
192 pp
0 7524 2168 9   *£17.99*

ACKNOWLEDGEMENTS

My sincere thanks to all who have supplied and allowed the use of photographs and especially to the *Express and Star* and to Don Stanton, former FA Cup final linesman, of Pemandos Publishing.

Thanks also to my late parents, Jean and Tom, who encouraged my love of Walsall Football Club; to my sister, Val, who has shared so many memorable games with me; and my wife, Judith, who has given marvellous secretarial support and has come to love Walsall Football Club almost as much as I do.

Finally, thanks to all the players, pressmen and fans who over the last fifty years have shared so many happy conversations on our favourite subject, Walsall Football Club.

Jimmy Walker – a stalwart Walsall custodian.

INTRODUCTION

The most difficult task for a book of this kind is that of choosing just 100 great players from the 1,042 who have represented Walsall in League games since 1888. To a fan like myself they are all heroes.

Certain criteria have been used to make the selection a little simpler. Anyone who has made over 250 appearances and or scored 50 or more goals is an obvious choice. So is anyone who went on to achieve fame at international level after leaving Walsall, players such as Bert Williams, Phil Parkes, and Allan Clarke. Then there are those who achieved memorable feats, such as Dave Massart's three hat-tricks in successive home games or Darren Byfield's extra-time match-winner in the play-off final to take Walsall back to Division One. A fascinating aspect of the hundred players chosen is that no fewer than eleven of them are goalkeepers – but then Walsall have usually had a first-rate last line of defence. Even so, many fine players have had to be omitted – it would have been quite easy to find 200 greats.

Total appearances and goals are given for each of the hundred 'greats' and in this connection 'other' competitions include the prewar Third Division Cup, post-war play-offs and the variously-labelled Associate Members, Freight Rover, Sherpa Van, Leyland Daf, Autoglass, Autowindscreen and LDV Vans competitions, not forgetting the Simod Cup, in which Walsall played just one game in 1988/89. Statistics are correct up to the end of the 2000/01 season.

My thanks to all the players who have given fans like myself so much pleasure – pleasure which has been relived in the writing of this book and which I hope will be experienced by all who read it.

Geoff Allman
August 2001

100 WALSALL GREATS

Gilbert Alsop	Frank Gregg	Lew Morgan
George Andrews	Teddy Groves	Fred Morris
Nick Atthey	Bill Guttridge	Kenny Mower
Steve Baines	Harry Haddington	Albert Mullard
Allan Baker	*Johnny Hancocks*	Albert Newman
Fred Barber	John Harris	Charle Ntamark
Stan Bennett	*Colin Harrison*	Martin O'Connor
Fred Biddlestone	Peter Hart	Richard O'Kelly
Alan Birch	Ken Hill	Granville Palin
Roger Boli	Ken Hodgkisson	*Phil Parkes*
Alan Boswell	*Sammy Holmes*	Don Penn
Bill Bradford	Roy John	David Preece
Alan Buckley	Stan Jones	Andy Rammell
Darren Byfield	Mick Kearns	Tim Rawlings
Brian Caswell	Dean Keates	Mark Rees
Phil Chapman	*David Kelly*	*Tony Richards*
Gary Childs	George Kirby	Stuart Rimmer
Trevor Christie	Mo Lane	Dave Serella
Allan Clarke	Jorge Latao	Craig Shakespeare
Nicky Cross	Jackie Lewis	Jack Shelton
Ron Crutchley	Kyle Lightbourne	Bill Sheppard
Joe Cunningham	*Doug Lishman*	Lee Sinnott
Don Dearson	Ron McDonald	Bill Skidmore
Miah Dennehy	Jimmy McMorran	*Colin Taylor*
Johnny Devlin	*Albert McPherson*	Adrian Viveash
Don Dorman	Peter McSevich	*Harry Wait*
Jimmy Dudley	Tony Macken	*Jimmy Walker*
Bill Evans	Norman Male	Henry Walters
Mick Evans	*Chris Marsh*	*Bert Williams*
Roy Faulkner	Dave Massart	*Dennis Wilshaw*
Graeme Forbes	Pedro Matias	Kevin Wilson
Reg Foulkes	George Meek	Bernie Wright
Bill Green	Irvine Methley	
Ron Green	Colin Methven	

The top 20, who appear here in italics, occupy two pages instead of the usual one.

Gilbert Alsop

Striker, 1931-1935 and 1938-1947

	First Team Appearances	Goals
Football League	195	151
FA Cup	21	13
Others	6	5
TOTAL	222	169

Walsall's greatest-ever striker was born in Frampton Cotterill, Bristol in 1908. He played for Latterbridge FC and Bath City, before linking up with Coventry City in 1929. He made his debut for the Bantams (as the Sky Blues were then known) against Crystal Palace in February 1930, but after scoring just 4 goals in 16 games he was one of several players whom manager Harry Storer allowed to move to Walsall in the early 1930s.

He arrived at Fellows Park in October 1931 and scored on his debut in a 2-0 win against Doncaster. Later that season, he got hat-tricks in the space of five days against Halifax and Accrington and ended the season with a tally of 15 goals in 29 games.

It was clear that Walsall had landed a major asset, but Gilbert went on to exceed all hopes. His finest hour came on 14 January 1933, when he played a major part in Walsall's 2-0 win over Arsenal, which still ranks as one of the greatest giant-killing acts of all time. After a goal-less first half, he headed home a Freddy Lee corner after the interval and a few minutes later hustled a young Arsenal defender into aiming a retaliatory kick at him. A penalty was awarded and Bill Sheppard (another former Coventry man) calmly netted from the spot.

A season later, Alsop got 40 goals in 43 games to set a new club record. Amazingly he bettered even that in 1934/5, with 48 goals in 52 games. It came as no surprise that Gilbert was on several clubs' shopping lists and in November 1935 he moved to West Brom to cover for W.G. Richardson. Alas, he played only one game for Albion and in May 1937 he moved on to Ipswich, who were then in the Southern League. He averaged a goal per game in his first season there, at the end of which they were elected to the Football League.

Ipswich's first away game, oddly enough, was at Walsall, where they won 1-0. Although Gilbert didn't score, Walsall realized how much they needed him back and two months later they secured his signature. It took him a few weeks to open his account but when he did so, the goals flowed again. In one spell the following April, he banged home 16 goals in 5 games, including four in a single game on two occasions.

Gilbert kept scoring during the war years, whether playing for Walsall (58 in 105 games) or when guesting for Leicester, Luton, Mansfield and Northampton. In the first post-war season he played in an FA Cup tie against Liverpool, but alas there was to be no

Gilbert Alsop in his later years as groundsman at Fellows Park. In the background is the Hillary Street End, where he scored against Arsenal in 1933.

repeat giant-killing, as the visitors won 5-2. Gilbert gave up first-team football in May 1947 and spent the next couple of seasons playing for and coaching the club's third team. He then spent some years as groundsman to a local firm, F.H. Lloyds – and in his forties still scored goals for them. Then, after serving a local playhouse as groundsman, he returned to Walsall's Fellows Park in that capacity. He retired in the 1970s and attended games for the rest of his days. Fans still practically queued up to talk to him and to hear his thoughts expressed in his lovely West Country accent. Gilbert died in April 1992, but older Walsall fans still speak of him with affection.

George Andrews

Striker 1973-1977

	First Team Appearances	Goals
Football League	159	38
FA Cup	14	2
FL Cup	4	0
TOTAL	177	40

Although he was over thirty when he signed for Walsall, George Andrews gave over four years' excellent service and figured in some of the most memorable games in the club's history.

Born in Dudley in 1942, George played his early football for Vono Sports and then had a short spell with Luton Town without breaking through into the first team. He returned to his native West Midlands and made a great impact with Lower Gornal Athletic, which brought League clubs flocking. It was Cardiff City who secured his signature in October 1965. He scored on his debut against Portsmouth and in just under two seasons scored 25 goals in 48 games. He played at different times as twin striker, alongside future Liverpool stalwart John Toshack and the young George Johnston, who was to have a short spell on loan to Walsall in 1970.

It was in 1967 that George Andrews moved to Southport, who were then in the Fourth Division. Again, he scored on his debut (against Barnsley), helping them to promotion at the end of the season and, two seasons later, Walsall experienced his opportunism at first hand when he got one of the goals in a Boxing Day 2-1 win over them.

After netting 41 goals in 117 games for Southport he moved to Shrewsbury in November 1969, yet again scoring on his debut, this time in a 1-1 draw against Orient. Just a week later he got both goals in a 3-2 defeat at Walsall. The Saddlers had another sample of his finishing in September 1971, when he got two of the Shrews' goals in a 4-1 win.

Andrews had totalled 56 goals in 136 games for Shrewsbury by the time he moved to Walsall in January 1973. Despite finishing on the losing side, he netted in both his first two games (at Grimsby and Wrexham). Although he didn't keep up this scoring rate in his first season and a half at Walsall, he really came good in 1974/75, playing in all 53 League and cup games and numbering amongst his 14 goals a splendid match-winning header that put Newcastle out of the FA Cup and Walsall into the fifth round for only the second time in their history.

During his four and a half seasons with Walsall, his nonchalant style and seemingly slender frame concealed a player of great staying power, with an eye for goal and outstanding ability in the air. Many fans were disappointed when, after scoring two goals at Peterborough and one against Bury right at the end of 1976/77, he was released during the summer. He continued to score regularly during spells with Worcester, Telford, Oldwinford, Tipton and Solihull as he played up to his mid-forties; he then turned out in charity games for several more years. George Andrews really was a striker who scored goals wherever he went.

Nick Atthey

Midfielder, 1963-1977

	First Team Appearances	Goals
Football League	439	17
FA Cup	42	0
FL Cup	21	1
TOTAL	502	18

Nick Atthey was one of Walsall's finest ever midfielders – being one of several of the discoveries of superscout Ron Jukes, who spent his whole career with Walsall.

Born in the Newcastle on Tyne area in 1946, just four days after Walsall had appeared in the Third Division (South) Cup final, Nick moved with his parents to the Coventry area in time to play for the Coventry Boys side which won the Birmingham and District Shield in 1961. Soon afterwards, he joined Walsall as an amateur and turned professional in 1963.

He was one of a splendid clutch of young players (Allan Clarke, Stan Bennett and Colin Harrison were amongst the others) who moved steadily into regular first-team places. He made his debut in a game at QPR right at the end of the 1963/64 season, just before Bill Harrison moved in as chairman and Ray Shaw as manager.

At this stage he played in 71 successive games, including the League Cup tie at West Brom in front of 41,000 fans, in which only a dubious offside decision robbed him of a goal that would have given Walsall the lead in a humdinger of a game. Later that same season, he was a member of the Walsall side that beat Stoke 2-0 at the Victoria Ground in the FA Cup with just ten men (Jimmy McMorran had been injured in those pre-substitue days).

Nick was troubled with injuries in the early 1970s but came back strongly to play in 51 of the club's 53 League and cup games in 1974/75, including the unforgettable FA Cup wins over Manchester United and Newcastle.

By the time he dropped out of League football in 1977, Nick had played in more games for Walsall than Colin Taylor – a tally that has since been exceeded only by Colin Harrison. Nick was just about the complete midfielder: strong in the tackle, a good user of the ball, exciting on the overlap and a great crosser, equally happy in an attacking or defensive role. After leaving Walsall, he played for Telford United and later for Rushall Olympic. He still lives in the Walsall area.

Nick (extreme left, back row) is pictured here with Walsall's 1971/72 line-up, when they finished in ninth place in the Third Division. During the course of the season, Bill Moore (third from left, second row) resigned as manager, and John Smith (second from left, second row) took over. This line-up is remarkable in that it contains not only Nick Atthey, but also Colin Taylor (second from left, back row) and Frank Gregg (second from left, second row) – all of whom played more than 400 games for Walsall.

Steve Baines

Central defender, 1980-1982

	First Team Appearances	Goals
Football League	48	5
FA Cup	2	0
TOTAL	50	5

Steve Baines was one of many much-travelled defenders to have played for Walsall over the years, but he is unique in being the only Walsall player to have later become a Football League referee.

Born in Newark in 1954, Steve joined Nottingham Forest from school and as a teenager played twice in their defence, before moving to Huddersfield in July 1975. He made a big impression in the course of 114 games in the Fourth Division and moved to Bradford City just before the transfer deadline in 1978. In both of his two full seasons at Valley Parade he was voted Player of the Year and he was also chosen for the PFA Fourth Division representative team in 1980.

Soon afterwards he moved to Walsall for a fee of £50,000, fixed by an independent tribunal. This was, at the time, a record for an outgoing transfer from Bradford City. He went straight into the Walsall defence but it was as a goal-snatcher that he first won the hearts of fans, netting a spectacular header in his first home game against Burnley and getting the winner in a 4-3 thriller against Carlisle just over a month later. In fact, in the four games

that season in which Steve scored, Walsall won – and these points were absolutely vital in a season in which they escaped relegation to the Fourth Division by just one point.

Steve was troubled with injury the following campaign and had a spell on loan to Bury around the turn of the year, but he returned to play in ten end-of-season games as Walsall again just avoided relegation. He moved to Scunthorpe as player-coach in the summer of 1982, played in 38 games in the following season and helped them to promotion from the Fourth Division.

From there it was on to Chesterfield, where he arrived in the summer of 1983 and went on to enjoy the most successful spell of his career as he captained the Spirites to the Fourth Division championship of 1984/85. His 153 games for them took his career tally close to the 500 mark and his 10 goals took his career tally past the 50 mark.

During 1987 and 1988, Steve played for Matlock, Afreton, Gainsborough and Burton, but an arthritic neck ended his playing days. He immediately took up refereeing and by 1995 he was on the Football League list. Since then he has taken charge of several Walsall games and has been well received by fans.

	First Team Appearances	Goals
Football League	137	31
FA Cup	17	3
FL Cup	10	2
TOTAL	164	36

Alan Baker was one of those joys of football fans, a skilful ball player who could also score goals. How sad that his career was ended by injury at the age of twenty-six, when he was just reaching his peak.

Born in Tipton in 1944, he quickly made his mark in schoolboy football, playing for both Staffordshire and Birmingham County Boys and being capped by England at both schoolboy and youth level. In the meantime he had linked up with Aston Villa and he played for them in the First Division in April 1961 when still only sixteen. He gained a regular place in 1962/63, playing on numerous occasions alongside Derek Dougan, but a broken arm the following season set him back and, although he played regular first-team football again in the second half of 1964/65, Villa were happy to release him in the summer of 1966, after he had scored just 17 goals in 109 matches.

Walsall therefore picked up a rare bargain at £10,000 and in his very first season, of 1966/67, he played in 50 games and scored 16 goals. Fans who saw it still talk of his remarkable goal in a League Cup win at Exeter, when he went past man after man to open the scoring. His delicacy of touch was revealed later that season, when he netted a perfect lob over the head of Oxford goalkeeper, Jim Barron.

Early the following season he got a match-winner at Shrewsbury that closely resembled the one at Exeter a year earlier. For the next few seasons it seemed that, as a midfield controller who had an eye for the spectacular goal, he would be one of the players around whom a Walsall promotion side would be built.

Sadly, in September 1970, tragedy struck as, not many minutes after he had scored the opening goal in a game against Tranmere, he suffered a serious knee injury. Despite brave efforts by himself and the medical men, he could never play football again.

Appropriately perhaps for one of the Saddlers' most skilful players, Alan then went into the leather trade in Walsall.

Fred Barber

Goalkeeper, 1986-91

	First Team Appearances	Goals
Football League	153	0
FA Cup	12	0
FL Cup	9	0
Others	15	0
TOTAL	189	0

This goalkeeper of many clubs was also a most colourful personality – and not just on account of the different hues of jersey that he wore. Never did he show his true colours more clearly than in his tremendous contribution to Walsall's 1987/88 promotion to the Second Division.

Born in Ferryhill in 1963, Fred spent his early days with Darlington, for whom he played 135 League games, before signing for Everton in March 1986. Just over half a year later, he moved to Walsall in search of first-team football. In the early days of the Terry Ramsden era, the Saddlers invested £100,000 in him – and he fully justified the fee.

Making his debut in a 4-1 win over Rotherham, Fred missed only one game for the rest of that season and helped Walsall to reach the fifth round of the FA Cup, where they had two replays against Watford. Then, in 1987/88 he played in all 61 League and cup games, including the playoff final against Bristol City, which was contested on a home and away basis. In fact, it was Fred's penalty shoot-out saves that earned Walsall home advantage for the third replay, which they won 4-0.

He missed only the last two games of Walsall's unhappy relegation season of 1988/89 and then, in the following campaign, found himself having to battle for his place with Ron Green, who had returned for a second spell. In search of first-team football, Barber had loan spells with Peterborough, Chester, Blackpool and Chester again, before moving to Peterborough for £25,000 in the summer of 1991. Though Fred had not played for Walsall for most of 1990/91, he returned to play in the last two games of that season and helped them to 4-0 and 2-0 wins over Aldershot and Blackpool respectively – in so doing they robbed the Seasiders of a promotion place.

While with Peterborough, he played a great part in their promotion via the play-offs in 1991/92 and then had loan spells with Chesterfield and Colchester. He moved to Luton in the summer of 1994, only to find himself on loan again to Peterborough and then to Ipswich and Blackpool.

In the summer of 1996 he moved to Birmingham, played once for them and then had a spell with Kidderminster in 1996/97. Since then he has served several clubs, as goalkeeping coach.

Although Fred served a total of ten different League clubs and was on the books of two others, his longest spell was at Walsall, where he is remembered not just for his wearing a face mask to get the crowd laughing, but for his splendid consistency and safe pair of hands.

Stan Bennett

Central defender and midfielder, 1963-1975

	First Team Appearances	Goals
Football League	386	12
FA Cup	33	1
FL Cup	19	0
TOTAL	438	13

This lionhearted defender, who figured equally effectively in midfield, was the personification of all the greatest qualities of Walsall players over the years, a one-club man whose every sinew was strained in each game he played.

Born in Birmingham in 1944, he was one of the many discoveries of former chief scout Ron Jukes. After skippering both Aston Boys and Birmingham Boys, Bennett graduated via the apprenticeship ranks to sign as a professional in 1962 and make his first-team debut in a 1-0 win at Notts County in October 1963. He also put in some powerful performances as an attacking wing-half before the end of that season and was an immediate hit with Walsall fans, who have always known a good club man when they see one.

Though former England international Trevor Smith was signed in the following season, he was never fully mobile after an injury. Stan made the central defensive position his own by the end of that campaign and in the next few seasons rarely missed a game. His greatest performances were probably in cup ties against West Brom (when he contained the twin spearhead of Jeff Astle and John Kay) and against Stoke (twice), when he played a major part in dramatic wins.

Between 1968 and 1972 he played mainly in midfield, as Stan Jones had returned to the club to play in defence. Stan Bennett's firm but fair tackling and occasional burst into attack continued to have the crowd roaring. He also snatched a few goals, none better than the fine volley with which he opened the scoring at Brighton in February 1972.

After Stan Jones' move to Kidderminster, Stan Bennett was back at the heart of the defence in the 1973, 1974 and 1975 seasons and was commended by Tommy Docherty (then manager of Manchester United) for his two titanic displays when Walsall first drew at Old Trafford and then beat United 3-2 at Fellows Park.

It was a great shock to fans when Stan was released at the end of the 1974/75 season. Some stayed away from games as a direct result. Stan, meanwhile, joined Nuneaton as player-manager and continued to manage them after a broken leg had virtually ended his playing career.

More recently he has worked as a building society branch manager in the south of England. It is sad that his dynamic approach and love of football have been lost to the game, though his nephew, Martyn Bennett, played for West Brom over 200 times in the 1980s.

Stan (centre) is pictured here with manager Bill Moore, on his left, and Nick Atthey, on his right. They are signing autographs for young fans during a 'meet the team' venture, sponsored by a local newspaper, in 1970.

Fred Biddlestone

Goalkeeper, 1929/30

	First Team Appearances	Goals
Football League	21	0
FA Cup	3	0
TOTAL	24	0

One of the many fine goalkeepers who have begun their League careers with Walsall, Fred Biddlestone was born in Dudley in 1906 and was an outfield player in his early days. He first played in goal for Moxley Wesleyans, Wednesbury Town, Sunbeam Motors and Bloxwich Strollers, before signing for Walsall in April 1929. He made his debut in the opening game of the following season at Gillingham and made an immediate impact.

He kept Harry Wait, who up to then had missed only one League game in six seasons, out of the team, and played like someone who had been in League football all his life. When he turned out for the FA Cup tie at Villa Park on 25 January 1930, it was only his twenty-third game for Walsall, but a gate of 74,626 saw his masterly display, which limited Villa's winning margin to 3-1.

He was destined to play only one more game for Walsall, as Villa came in with a bid of £1,750 (a remarkably high fee for a goalkeeper in those days) and just four days after playing in Walsall's 1-0 home win over Luton, he played in Villa's 2-1 home defeat by Burnley. He seemed to be the natural successor to Ben Olney (who later had a spell with Walsall) but then, after being injured in a pre-match kick-about in November 1931, lost his place to Harry Morton and did not regain it until 1936.

Fred played a major role in Villa's promotion from the Second Division in 1937/38 and played fairly regularly in First Division in 1938/39, before losing his place to the young Joe Rutherford. He moved to Mansfield in the summer of 1939, played in the three games of that season before war broke out and then guested regularly for Walsall during the early war years.

In the course of 70 wartime games, he figured in the remarkable 11-4 win over Notts County in November 1940 and the 10-3 win over West Brom in May 1941.

Fred later ran a boarding house in Blackpool, where he was always pleased to meet Walsall fans who remembered him affection for his outstanding displays for Walsall, both at the beginning and end of his career.

Alan Birch
Midfielder, 1973-1979

	First Team Appearances	Goals
Football League	171	23
FA Cup	11	0
FL Cup	9	1
TOTAL	191	24

Alan Birch became Walsall's youngest ever Football League player when he went on as substitute against Bristol Rovers in March 1973 aged just 16 years and 209 days.

Born in West Bromwich in August 1956, he is the older brother of Paul Birch, who later played for Aston Villa, Wolves and Walsall. Chief scout Ron Jukes steered him towards Fellows Park after he had played several trial games for West Brom. He was still on amateur forms when he made several more appearances before the end of season 1972/73, being still too young to sign as a professional.

He earned a regular place in the following season, scored several opportunist goals, and was still only nineteen when he played in the memorable wins over Manchester United and Newcastle United, early in 1975.

Alan scored a fair number of goals, getting a hat-trick in a 5-3 win at Peterborough in May 1977 and, in what proved to be his last season at Fellows Park, he got 9 goals in 1978/79. He was helped by the fact that he had taken over as penalty 'king' after Alan Buckley's move to Birmingham.

One of his last games for Walsall was in a goal-less draw at Chesterfield and four months later the Spireites (managed then by former Walsall coach Arthur Cox) signed him. He played more of a front-running role and got 45 goals in 129 games for them. He moved to Wolves in 1981 and then moved at regular intervals to Barnsley, back to Chesterfield, and then on to Rotherham, Scunthorpe and Stockport. At the age of thirty-four he dropped out of League football and played in quick succession for Shepshed Charterhouse, Matlock and Frickley Athletic.

In his long career, Alan scored over a hundred goals, covered hundreds of miles with his tireless running and in more recent years has worked as a publican.

Alan is typical of the numerous busy little midfielders who have served Walsall with distinction over the years. He followed in the footsteps of Nick Atthey and Ray Train, and was succeeded by David Preece and Dean Keates.

	First Team Appearances	Goals
Football League	41	12
FA Cup	4	4
FL Cup	6	2
Others	6	6
TOTAL	57	24

This quicksilver striker was with Walsall for only one season, but he will always be remembered by those who saw him and regretted that he was the wrong side of thirty when he came to Bescot.

Born on the Ivory Coast in June 1965, Roger was an under-21 French international early in his career, but no one was sure quite what Walsall were getting when he was signed on a free transfer from Lens in the summer of 1997. He missed most of the pre-season games, but manager Jan Sorensen put him straight into the team for the opening League game at Chesterfield. He looked rather small at just 5ft 7in as he ran out, and travelling fans reserved judgment at the end of a 3-1 defeat; but back at Bescot three days later, he first worried fans with his over-elaboration but then had them roaring with a stunning overhead kick.

Just over a fortnight later they shouted his praises, as he not only netted another overhead kick against Southend but went on to get a hat-trick, Walsall's first in a League game for three years. Soon he had scored in four games in a row and was justifying the tag of being (allegedly) the highest-paid player in Walsall's history. However, almost inevitably he got increasing attention from ruthless defenders. Things went badly wrong in a game with Wrexham when Roger opened the scoring and

then suffered a series of fouls, most of which went unpunished. Finally, after he had been elbowed in the face, he argued with the referee and was sent off.

Things were never quite the same again but he did get a goal in the 5-1 FA Cup defeat in front of a 54,669 gate at Old Trafford. Though he got only one more goal in the last three months of the season, Roger was second highest scorer in the Second Division and was selected by the PFA for the season's Second Division team.

He moved on to Dundee United during the following close season and had short spells with both them and Bournemouth before returning to France. The memories of his ability to turn on the ball and flash in a shot from any angle still live on.

Alan Boswell

Goalkeeper, 1961-1963

	First Team Appearances	Goals
Football League	66	0
FA Cup	5	1
FL Cup	1	0
TOTAL	72	0

Alan Boswell was spectacular, controversial and unpredictable, but on his day was a skilful and brave goalkeeper and one of the many home-grown Walsall custodians over the years.

Born in Wednesbury in 1943, Alan played for South East Staffordshire Schoolboys and graduated from the Walsall junior ranks to make his first-team debut as an eighteen-year-old against Norwich in November 1961, in their first season back in the Second Division after an absence of sixty years. He immediately won the hearts of the fans by leaping to punch away a cross into a crowded goal-mouth and then diving to turn away a powerful shot that seemed to be going inside a post.

Walsall won the game 5-0 and Alan held his place, despite both John Christie and Keith Ball being on Walsall's books at the time. In fact, he missed only one game in the next season and a half. Two of his heroic performances were in a 2-2 draw at Fulham in the FA Cup and in a 1-0 win at Chelsea as Walsall battled bravely against relegation.

Tragedy struck in the final game of 1962/63 when, needing just one point from the final game against Charlton in order to stay up, Walsall's first attempt to play the game was abandoned because of a half-time thunderstorm. Then, when the game was replayed Alan suffered a cracked cheekbone early in the match and the Saddlers lost 2-1.

During the following close season, Boswell had a difference of opinion with chairman Ernie Thomas and moved to Shrewsbury, who had just lost their goalkeeper Paul Miller (himself a former Walsall junior) in a drowning tragedy. Alan was still only twenty and he went on to give great service to the Shrews, playing in several outstanding cup runs in the course of over 250 games – in one game against Walsall he played bravely up front after breaking a collarbone in a collision.

Ronnie Allen signed him for Wolves in September 1968, but after just 10 games (in one of which he saved a penalty at Chelsea) he was released by Ronnie Allen's successor, Bill McGarry. He then spent three seasons with Bolton and two with Port Vale, conceding an own goal in one game against Walsall when he 'lost' a cross in the floodlights.

He then had a short spell with Blackburn without breaking through into the first team and ended his career with Oswestry in the mid-1970s. Since then he has worked in the one-armed bandit business and his son, Matthew, has played in goal for Kidderminster and Bilston in recent years.

No one who saw him play will ever forget Alan Boswell's speed from his goal to beat an opposing striker to the ball or his readiness to react when roughed up by larger opponents.

Bill Bradford

Midfielder, 1926-1938

	First Team Appearances	Goals
Football League	318	21
FA Cup	24	0
Others	9	1
TOTAL	351	22

Bill Bradford was the only Walsall player before the Second World War to play in fourteen consecutive seasons and he had extensive experience in both sections of the Third Division.

Born in Peggs Green, Leicestershire in 1900, Bill was the younger brother of Joe Bradford, the striker who scored over 250 goals for Birmingham and won 12 England caps. Bill followed his brother to St Andrews in the early 1920s, but failed to break through into the first team and moved to Brighton in 1924. He played only three first-team games, however, and moved to Preston in the summer of 1925, playing just once in North End's Second Division side before joining Walsall in the summer of 1926.

He went straight into the first team and in the opening game of the 1926/27 season made an impressive debut, getting the equalizer in a 2-2 draw at Doncaster. Oddly enough he didn't score again for a year and a half, but when he did so it was worth waiting for, as he netted twice in a 7-0 hammering of Coventry in February 1928.

Bradford was an ever-present in the number six shirt in the 1929/30 season, his most memorable game being the fourth round FA Cup tie at Villa Park when Walsall's eleven heroes went down 3-1 in front of 74,626 fans, thousands of whom had walked from Walsall. Although playing mainly in midfield, Bill was always ready to fill a gap in defence or up front and he was a little unlucky to miss the famous 1933 FA Cup win over Arsenal. Just three weeks after that historic day he was back in the side and a year later he became player-coach. However, he continued to play regularly and in February 1937 featured in what was his 300th League game – appropriately enough at Brighton, where he had made his Football League debut twelve years earlier.

His last game was an unhappy one – a 5-1 home defeat by Southend in January 1938. He returned to the family farm, leaving behind many memories of a player who had battled away for Walsall Football Club for fourteen seasons and had had a spell as captain. An example of his longevity as a player is that in his first game he had enjoyed alongside pre-First World War Fulham player, Jimmy Torrance, and in his last game was in front of post-Second World War international goalkeeper Bert Williams.

23

Alan Buckley
Striker, 1973-1985

	First Team Appearances	Goals
Football League	419	177
FA Cup	31	14
FL Cup	31	14
Others	3	0
TOTAL	484	205

Alan Buckley ranks alongside pre-war hero Gilbert Alsop and 1950s and '60s sharpshooters Tony Richards and Colin Taylor as one of the greatest goalscorers ever to play for Walsall.

Born in Mansfield in 1951, Alan graduated via the apprenticeship ranks to sign as a professional for Nottingham Forest in 1968. He made his debut in a 6-1 defeat at Tottenham and scored just once in 19 games over five seasons, though he was a well-known figure in Central League football during those years, his fair hair attracting attention amongst the sparse crowds up and down the country.

That being the case, Ronnie Allen did well to secure his signature during his short spell as manager in 1973. Alan's debut was ordinary enough – a 2-0 defeat at Exeter on the opening day of the 1973/74 season, but just four days later he got a hat-trick in a 6-1 hammering of Shrewsbury in the League Cup and fans began singing his name.

That singing continued with very few gaps for over a decade. Alan played in every game in his first three seasons with Walsall – a remarkable achievement in itself, when strikers get a fair amount of painful attention from no-nonsense defenders. What is more, he scored at a rate few players have equalled in the last thirty years. One of his greatest feats was scoring two goals (one from the penalty spot) in the FA Cup replay win over Manchester United in January 1975. Then, in the following season, his 35 League and cup goals included two of his best ever in the 2-0 win over Brighton just before Christmas and three hat-tricks in just over a month in February and March.

Many fans thought the end of the world had come when Alan moved to Birmingham for £170,000 in August 1978, and Walsall were relegated at the end of the season. He scored just 8 goals in 29 games for the Blues but one of them (against Wolves at Molineux on Boxing Day 1978) was one of the finest of his career – a powerful diagonal overhead kick.

What joy for Walsall fans in the summer of 1979 when Alan (who had had a short spell as caretaker a year earlier) returned to Fellows Park as player-manager – and at the same fee for which they had sold him a few months earlier. This was one of chairman Ken Wheldon's shrewdest moves, for Alan led Walsall to promotion at the first attempt – and got 18 goals himself.

The next couple of seasons were a struggle,

Alan Buckley celebrates one of his many goals at Walsall's Fellows Park Ground.

as Alan shared managerial responsibilities for the first part of 1981/82 and then played under Neil Martin for the second half of the season. Walsall managed to stay up, however, and with Alan back in sole charge in 1982/83, his goalscoring form returned as he played in every game and scored 15 goals.

From 1983/84 he played mainly as a substitute and his last appearance as a player was going on as substitute for Richard O'Kelly in a 2-1 win over Preston on Boxing Day 1984. This was just ten months after the dramatic run to the semi-final of the Milk Cup, in which Walsall beat Arsenal at Highbury and drew with Liverpool at Anfield. Some of the football they played during this period was amongst the best ever played by Walsall teams, but in successive seasons, promising promotion runs faded after Christmas. In 1986, Alan was replaced as manager by Tommy Coakley, as new chairman Terry Ramsden literally flew in like a breath of fresh air.

Alan then played briefly for Stourbridge and Tamworth, managed Kettering, Grimsby (twice) and West Brom and near the end of 2000/01 took charge of Lincoln. As a manager he has had mixed fortunes, his greatest triumph being that of taking Grimsby from the old Fourth Division to Division One between 1990 and 1992. As an opportunist, his figures speak for themselves – and one wonders whether a Walsall striker will ever again do what Alan did in scoring more than ten goals in each of eight successive seasons. His record indicates that a striker need not be of large proportions, for Alan was just 5ft 8in in his goalscoring glory days.

Darren Byfield

Striker, 2000-present

	First Team Appearances	Goals
Football League	40	9
FA Cup	3	0
FL Cup	4	1
Others	4	1
TOTAL	51	11

Whatever else he achieves in his subsequent career, Darren Byfield has already won an indelible place in Walsall's history by dint of the spectacular match-winner that he scored in the Division Two play-off final in May 2001.

Born in Birmingham in 1976, Darren attracted attention as an Aston Villa trainee in the early 1990s, when he first revealed that great crowd-pleasing quality of being a striker with real pace. He signed professionally for Villa in 1994 and made his first-team debut right at the end of December 1996, in a 1-1 draw at Leeds. He made a number of substitute appearances that season and then in November 1998 was loaned to Preston, scored on his debut against Burnley before picking up an injury before his loan spell was up.

In 1999/2000 he had further loan spells at Northampton, Cambridge and Blackpool and then in June 2000 joined Walsall on a free transfer. He went straight into the first team and netted twice in his first home game against Oldham.

For the rest of the season he was used almost equally as a striker to aim to try and give his side a flying start, or a substitute to aim at changing the course of a game. In both roles he had considerable success. Amongst his most valuable goals were the one he got with his first touch after going on against Notts County in September and his late headed equalizer at Bournemouth in February.

Even when he didn't score, his pace kept defenders on edge and it was fitting that after over two months without a goal he achieved what he had dreamed of doing some weeks earlier by turning suddenly on the ball and cracking home a twenty-yard shot at the Millennium Stadium to take Walsall into Division One.

In Division One, he is proving to be a handful for experienced defenders, and at the time of publication, he is one of the key figures in Walsall's bid to hold onto their hard-won place.

	First Team Appearances	Goals
Football League	400	17
FA Cup	25	2
FL Cup	29	0
Others	4	0
TOTAL	458	19

Brian Caswell not only stands in seventh position in the all-time list of Walsall appearances but he is also one of the finest utility men in the club's history.

Born in Wednesbury in 1956, he attended Mesty Croft Junior School, where former Walsall chief scout Ron Jukes was headmaster. Therefore, when he showed outstanding promise as a footballer, there was no doubting where he would end up after leaving Wood Green Secondary School. As a Walsall apprentice his progress was so swift that even before signing professionally in September 1973, he had already made his League debut, in a 3-2 win over Chesterfield in the previous February. He played on the left flank of the defence, opposite veteran Frank Gregg (another Ron Jukes discovery), who was then in his last season at Fellows Park.

Early in the following season, Brian gave an outstanding display in a League Cup tie against Manchester City and, though he did not win a regular first-team place until 1976/77, he did well whenever he played. Although he settled into the number three shirt on the left flank of the defence, he had by that time also had experience as a central defender, a midfielder, a right-flank defender and a left-flank attacker.

He was voted Player of the Season in 1976/77 and though he had the bad luck to break an ankle in the following campaign, he was quickly back again. In the 1979/80 promotion season he missed only one of Walsall's 52 League and cup games, and also netted six goals. By the time he was figuring in the 1983/84 run to the Milk Cup semi-final, Brian was playing on the right flank of the defence. He had by that time had a successful benefit, when he got one of the goals in a 3-3 draw against West Brom and it seemed that he might go on to set up an all-time Walsall appearance record.

Sadly, however, he was allowed to move to Doncaster in the summer of 1985, still the right side of thirty. Not for the first time, fans were not happy at a popular player not being retained. The reported £20,000 seemed a paltry fee.

It seemed that Brian had dropped on his feet when, just a few months after moving to Doncaster, he followed manager Billy Bremner to Leeds. Sadly, however, he was to play only nine games for them as he was troubled by a series of injuries.

His last-ever League game was, oddly

Brian Caswell leaves an opponent beaten and dispirited as he surges forward.

enough, for Wolves in a 2-1 win at Cardiff in the Fourth Division in January 1987, with Brian wearing the number six shirt in which he had started his career.

Since then he has had spells on the coaching staffs of Birmingham City, Telford and Shrewsbury, while continuing to participate in charity games. He has been a popular visitor back at Walsall in various social events as the twenty-first century got underway.

	First Team Appearances	Goals
Football League	63	36
FA Cup	5	3
TOTAL	68	39

Phil was a perfect example of a one-season wonder, but those who saw the way he banged home the goals in 1948/49 will never forget the tremendous impact he made when it seemed that he just couldn't stop scoring.

Born in Chasetown in 1925, he first attracted attention just after the war, when he scored lots of goals for Cannock Chase Colliery. Harry Hibbs was then Walsall manager and, having tried for some months to find a replacement for prolific Dave Massart, he gave the young Chapman a trial. While still on amateur forms, Phil netted twice in Walsall's reserve game at Dudley and once against West Brom 'A' early in the 1948/49 season and, on the strength of these feats, Harry gave Phil the chance to show his mettle in the first team.

Accordingly, he ran out for the home game against Reading on 25 September 1948, fearing that he would not stand the pace, having not played amongst full-time professionals before. He need not have worried, for after going close in the very first minute he scored just after the interval and, in general, put himself about intelligently. Walsall not only won that game 2-0, but a week later they won 3-2 at Crystal Palace, with Phil on the mark again.

Then, just before Christmas, he netted twice against Norwich, one of the goals being the neatest of overhead flicks after a Lew Tinkler shot had come back off the post. In the following February and March he equalled the feats of two of Walsall's greatest strikers, Gilbert Alsop and Dave Massart, by getting hat-tricks in successive games against Crystal Place and Exeter. The Exeter strike was particularly noteworthy, as much of the game was played in a blizzard and one of the goals came when, in Phil's own words, 'I hit the ball from just inside the Exeter half without being able to see the visitors' goal.' It just flew into the net and visiting 'keeper Bert Hoyle said after the game that he just hadn't seen what proved to be the match-winner go by.

Phil's tally by the end of the season was 28 goals in 33 games, but sadly he never struck that sort of form again. He got just 8 goals and 3 goals respectively in the next two seasons, though he never failed to give of his best. Somehow the ball just didn't run for him, though he continued to score regularly in the reserves as he was in and out of the first team.

Many fans felt that he might have 'come again', but in 1951 he was released and linked up with Weymouth in the Southern League. For a time he played alongside Dave Massart, who had been even more prolific during his short spell with Walsall.

Later, Phil returned to the Midlands and joined Walsall police force. He scored many goals for their football team before a broken ankle effectively ended his playing career. He was often to be seen on duty at Walsall games after that and he continued to take an interest in his old club right up to his death in 1997. 'Shoot on sight' was Phil's motto and on the days when this came off, how the crowd roared.

Gary Childs
Midfielder, 1983-1987

	First Team Appearances	Goals
Football League	131	17
FA Cup	30	2
FL Cup	16	2
Others	7	2
TOTAL	184	23

Gary Childs was a neat little midfielder who packed a tremendous shot and was one of the stars of Walsall's run to the Milk Cup semi-final in 1984.

Born in Kings Heath in 1964, he won 4 England youth caps while an apprentice with West Brom but he played only three first-team games for The Hawthorns club before linking up with Walsall in 1983. He came initially on loan, making his first-team debut in a 1-0 win at Rotherham in October 1983, when another ex-Albion man, Ally Brown, got the winner from a penalty.

A few weeks later Gary got his first goal for the club – and what a goal, as a twenty-yard shot whizzed home in the last minute to win a third round League Cup tie against Shrewsbury. Gary was in the side which proceeded to win at Arsenal and Rotherham and to pull off a 2-2 draw at Liverpool in the first leg of the semi-final.

Gary actually missed out on the second leg, which Liverpool won 2-0, but for the next three seasons he continued to be a crowd-pleaser with his neat footwork, constructive ability and occasional spectacular goal. It was in what proved to be his last season at Fellows Park that he enjoyed most success as a sharp-shooter – in Tommy Coakley's first season in charge Gary did more shooting and bagged 8 goals, including two each in the home games against Rotherham and Darlington respectively.

He moved to Birmingham in the summer of 1987 and after two seasons with them rejoined his former Walsall boss, Alan Buckley, at Grimsby. Childs was a key figure in the side that went from the Fourth Division to the Second Division in successive seasons, 1989/90 and 1990/91. By the time he left Blundell Park in 1997, and had spells with Wisbech Town and Boston United, Gary had played over 500 League and cup games for his four clubs – not a bad record for such a slightly-built player who stood just 5ft 7in high and weighed just 10½ stone.

Gary was one of a number of Walsall players over the years whose diminutive stature concealed a tremendously powerful shot, that thrilled fans and surprised opponents.

Trevor Christie
Striker, 1986-89

	First Team Appearances	Goals
Football League	99	22
FA Cup	12	4
FL Cup	5	1
Others	12	5
TOTAL	128	32

Trevor Christie was the sort of battling striker every manager prefers to have on his own side rather than the opposition's – and Trevor served a variety of managers in a career that took him to seven Football League clubs. Born in Newcastle in 1959, he served his apprenticeship with Leicester City and in 1978/79 was their leading scorer, albeit with only 8 goals. Then, when still only twenty, he moved to Notts County and played a prominent part in their sensational climb into the old First Division in 1981. When Leicester joined them there in 1983, he welcomed them by netting a hat-trick at Filbert Street.

Brian Clough signed him for Nottingham Forest in the summer of 1984, but Christie stayed there only just over half a season before moving to Derby and helping them to promotion from the Third Division in 1986. At that point he moved to Manchester City but, just two months into 1986/87, Tommy Coakley signed him for Walsall as he sought to beef up the Saddlers' attack.

Trevor did just that with his powerful running, ability to shield the ball and opportunism with both head and feet. He scored on his debut at Middlesbrough and three days later netted again in a 4-1 home win over Rotherham. Later that season, he starred in the fifth round FA Cup tie against Watford that went to three games. He netted a penalty equalizer at Fellows Park and then got two of the goals in the sensational 4-4 draw at Vicarage Road.

In the following season he linked up with David Kelly in Walsall's promotion win, scoring in the play-off semi-final against his former club, Notts County, and in the final against Bristol City. He also played a big part in David's tally of 28 goals by creating space for him. Then, as Walsall struggled in the old Second Division and finances became tight, he moved to Mansfield in March 1989 and had two good seasons with them, taking his career tally of League and cup goals well past the 150 mark.

Later, Christie had spells with Kettering, VS Rugby, Hucknall Town and Arnold Town before an Achilles tendon injury ended his playing career in his mid-thirties. 'Have boots, will travel and score goals' could well have been the maxim of this powerfully-built striker.

Allan Clarke
Striker, 1963-1966

	First Team Appearances	Goals
Football League	72	41
FA Cup	5	4
FL Cup	5	1
TOTAL	82	49

Possibly the greatest of former chief scout Ron Jukes's many discoveries, Allan Clarke went on to win 19 England caps and to star for the Leeds team of the 1970s which won a host of domestic and European honours.

Born in Willenhall in 1946, Allan was one of five brothers to play League football (four of them for Walsall) and represented Birmingham and South East Staffordshire Schools before linking up with Walsall as an apprentice in 1961 and as a professional in 1963. He made his debut in a 1-1 draw with Reading in October 1963 and won a regular place in the following season, netting his first hat-trick against Reading almost exactly a year after making his debut against them and going on to score 23 of Walsall's 55 goals that season.

An extra dimension was added to his game the following summer when Walsall signed the experienced striker George Kirby from Swansea. The pair formed one of the best dual spearheads Walsall have known, with George having the nous and the power and Allan the enthusiasm and eye for an opening with head or foot.

Allan also had the coolness from the penalty spot that saw him convert a last-minute League Cup winner against QPR and a vital second goal in a 2-0 FA Cup win at Stoke – with only ten men for much of the game. Allan's goal tally was 23 in 31 goals that season when, just before transfer deadline date, he joined Fulham in March 1966.

At £37,500 (the biggest fee Walsall had received up to then) he was a real giveaway and after two good seasons at Craven Cottage he cost Leicester a British record at that time of £150,000. In his one season at Filbert Street he got the goal that took them to the FA Cup final – in which he was voted Man of the Match, despite being on the losing side, the Foxes going down to Manchester City.

In the summer of 1969 the British record was beaten again, as Allan moved to Leeds for £165,000. In his nine years at Elland Road he got the winner in the 1972 FA Cup final, won a First Division Championship medal in 1974 and also helped Leeds win the European Fairs Cup (forerunner of the UEFA Cup) in 1971.

In the course of 19 games for England he scored 10 goals, including the penalty equalizer against Poland in October 1973.

All in all, he got 151 goals in 366 games for Leeds and after joining Barnsley as player-manager in the summer of 1978 he took them

Allan chats with former Walsall chairman, Bill Harrison, at Fellows Park. Former England manager, Alf Ramsay (in his pre-knighthood days), looks on.

to promotion in his first season there. 1980 saw him back at Leeds, this time as manager. He stayed for two years, after which came spells in charge of Scunthorpe (whom he took to promotion from the Fourth Division in 1983), Barnsley (again) and Lincoln.

More recently he has worked for a Scunthorpe steel firm, combining this with public relations work for Leeds and after-dinner speaking. He made a most memorable return to Walsall in the latter part of 2000 when he spoke at a Sportsman's Evening. He met up again with many of his former Walsall colleagues, and chatted freely with fans, who remembered him rivalling Jimmy Greaves as a finisher who rarely missed a chance. Don Revie knew what he was saying when he labelled him 'Sniffer'.

Nicky Cross

Striker, 1985-1988

	First Team Appearances	Goals
Football League	109	45
FA Cup	13	4
FL Cup	10	2
Others	7	1
TOTAL	139	52

Nicky Cross was one of many players over the years to make the short journey from West Bromwich Albion, where opportunities for him were limited, and make the most of having a regular first-team place with Walsall.

Born in Birmingham in 1961, Nicky played for a team called Woodbank Albion before joining West Brom at the time when Ron Atkinson was manager. He made his first-team debut as substitute in a game at Old Trafford in April 1981 and in fact 40 of his 119 games for Albion over the next four years were as substitute. He also got 19 goals, but it was after moving to Walsall in the summer of 1985 that the goals really flowed.

He got the opening goal on his debut in a 3-2 win at Bristol City in August 1985, scored in both legs of the Milk Cup win over Wolves and missed only three games in that first season at Fellows Park, scoring 24 goals. He got another 19 in the following season, one of them in the remarkable 4-4 FA Cup draw at Watford. He got his first hat-trick in the 5-2 win against Rotherham in January 1988, but was then taken off by Tommy Coakley, as the young Chris Marsh got his first taste of League football.

This upset the crowd, who were looking for more goals from Nicky that day as he was really on form, and they were less pleased still when, after just two more games, Nicky joined Leicester for £80,000. Walsall duly got promotion in the following May, but fans still looked longingly at the way Nicky continued to score goals for Leicester, and later for Port Vale as they went up to Division One in 1994. Nicky ended his League career at Hereford in 1994 and has since been active in the non-League scene as a manager.

At 5ft 9in, Nicky Cross was small for a striker and he carried little weight, but he was a fine opportunist and scored goals for all the teams for whom he played. He was an all-round player with the ability to shield the ball, turn in a tight situation and bustle as required.

In 2001, Nicky was manager of Redditch United in the Doctor Martens League. He has now completed twenty years of involvement with Midlands soccer, at various levels.

Ron Crutchley

Midfielder, 1945-1949

	First Team Appearances	Goals
Football League	62	4
FA Cup	9	0
TOTAL	71	4

Ask any Walsall fan aged over sixty at the turn of the century who they consider to have comprised the best-ever half-back line (as midfield operators were once known) they remember from Walsall teams over the years and the odds are that they will respond immediately with 'Crutchley, Foulkes and Newman' – the threesome with which Walsall kicked off normal divisional football again in 1946, after seven years of emergency wartime football.

Ron Crutchley, who played in the number four shirt in those days, was born in Walsall in 1922. He attracted the attention of Walsall Football Club, as did several of his contemporaries, while playing for Hillary Street Old Boys, managed by Gil Bromley. Crutchley's first game in the claret and blue of Walsall (their colours in those days) was a wartime one at Wrexham in March 1945.

He held his place for the rest of that season and then missed only two games in 1945/46, a transitional campaign in which Walsall reached the final of the Third Division (South) Cup and lost 1-0 to Bournemouth at Stamford Bridge. Ron played a full part in that memorable cup run with his firm tackling and use of the ball. Not the least of his attributes was his determined appearance, which belied a quiet, modest personality.

He played regularly in 1946/47 but lost his place to Henry Walters at the start of 1947/48.

However, he came back as an emergency striker to score a valuable goal in an FA Cup replay against Norwich and it was this readiness to have a go in any role for the good of the team that endeared him to fans. It was while playing as an emergency striker that he was injured in an Easter Saturday game at Watford in March 1948 and he missed the start of the following season.

Then, in January 1949, he was brought back into midfield with Henry Walters moving into the defence as Walsall pulled off a major FA Cup shock by winning at Fulham. For the rest of his time at Fellows Park he alternated between right-flank and left-flank midfield duties, with an occasional outing up front. He suffered a twisted knee in a Good Friday game against Swindon in April 1950 and in the close season moved to Shrewsbury, who had just been elected to the Football League.

He did much to help establish the Shrews and played over 150 games for them in the next four seasons. Even so, he always regretted leaving Walsall. Later, he had a spell with Telford United and then worked in the family toys and wholesale business in Littleton Street.

Sadly, Ron died at the early age of sixty-five, after a long illness, but he is remembered as one of the many Walsall-born and bred players who have been excellent professionals and real 'salt of the earth' characters in the eyes of fans.

Joe Cunningham
Goalkeeper, 1932-1934

	First Team Appearances	Goals
Football League	49	0
FA Cup	4	0
TOTAL	53	0

Joe Cunningham was certainly the man for a big occasion and has his place in Walsall's history by dint of that 1933 win over Arsenal and in Dartford's history because he figured in their FA Cup win over Cardiff in 1936.

Born in Dundee in 1904, Joe played just one game for Aberdeen (a 4-1 defeat at Hibernian) before trying his luck in the Football League with Newport County in 1925. He played just two games for Newport in 1925/26 but, after joining QPR in the following summer, he soon established himself in a Rangers side playing in the Third Division (South). Although he was on the wrong end of 3-1 and 4-0 defeats at Walsall during the next few years, he was quickly snapped up by Saddlers' boss Bill Slade when he became available in the summer of 1932, after 174 first-team appearances for the London club.

He made his debut in a 1-0 home win in the opening game of the new season and played in all 46 of the club's League and cup games, in one of the most memorable seasons in the club's history. Of the nine clean sheets that he kept, the most remarkable was in the FA Cup win over Arsenal. His save from Cliff Bastin early in the game gave his side the encouragement to battle for their very lives and the rest is now history.

In the following season he lost his place after a 4-2 home defeat by Halifax in October and such was the form of Peter McSevich, newly signed from Coventry, that Cunningham played just one more game and moved to York City in the close season. There he was again ever-present in his one and only season at Bootham, 1934/35. He had the satisfaction of helping his side do the double over Walsall, who were by that time fielding only five of the side which had beaten Arsenal.

Joe later played for Folkestone and Dartford and, while with the latter, figured in another FA Cup sensation, when they beat Cardiff 3-0 in November 1935 and gave First Division Derby a run for their money before going down 3-2.

Joe was the classic build for a goalkeeper – 6ft tall and 11½ stone and, though he made the odd slip in League games, he had that happy knack of rising to the big occasion.

	First Team Appearances	Goals
Football League	51	13
FA Cup	1	0
TOTAL	52	13

This former Welsh international was nearly thirty-six when he came to Walsall, but for a season and a half played in a variety of positions and always looked the part as he helped the club steer clear of having to apply for re-election.

Born in the Welsh town of Ynysybul in 1914, he won Welsh amateur international caps before linking up with Birmingham City in 1934. He played initially as an inside forward, but went on to do well in midfield and defence. He was capped 3 times by Wales before the war and won another 15 wartime caps when he was in a reserved occupation as an electrical engineer.

He also played regularly for the Blues during hostilities and guested for Northampton, Nottingham Forest, Wrexham and West Brom. He played on a number of occasions against Walsall during the war years and in November 1942 got a hat-trick in a 4-3 thriller. Including wartime games, Don played 202 goals for the Blues and scored 42 goals.

He moved on to Coventry in February 1947 and was in the Bantams' (as they were then known) team in January 1948 when they beat Walsall 2-1 in an FA Cup tie in front of 34,000 fans at Highfield Road. Then, in March 1950, Dearson moved to Walsall at a time when they were in the Third Division (South) danger zone. In his opening game, against League leaders, Notts County, he impressed from the first minute, Walsall fans being thrilled by the neat footwork and long throws of such a big man. He laid on the first two goals in a 3-3 draw.

In the final game of that season, he calmly netted two powerful shots against Crystal Palace to ensure that Walsall avoided a re-election application. In the following season he played up front, in midfield and both at the heart of the defence and on the left flank of defence and still managed to score 10 goals to be equal topscorer with Jack Winter.

In 1951 he moved on to Nuneaton and then had a short spell with Bilston, before becoming an employee of British Leyland and also running his own grocery business. Don died on Christmas Eve 1990, leaving behind memories of possibly the most versatile player ever to wear the Walsall colours.

Miah Dennehy

Winger, 1975-1978

	First Team Appearances	Goals
Football League	128	22
FA Cup	13	0
FL Cup	10	0
TOTAL	151	22

Miah Dennehy was the sort of exciting winger who really excited the crowd, and on his day he was also a lethal finisher.

Born in Cork in 1950, Miah (whose full name was Jeremiah) played Gaelic football as a teenager and went on to play for Cork Hibernian against Waterford in the Irish Cup final of 1972. A few weeks later he won the first of his 10 Republic of Ireland caps and in February 1973 he moved to Nottingham Forest, making his debut for them in a 2-1 win against Preston two months later.

In just over two seasons at the City Ground he played in 46 games and scored 4 goals, but a few months after Brian Clough had taken over, Dennehy moved to Walsall for a reported £10,000. There he linked up with former Forest player Dougie Fraser, who was by then manager of Fellows Park. He made his debut in a goal-less draw at Peterborough in the opening game of the 1975/76 season and missed only one game all season, scoring 8 goals himself and providing plenty of crosses for Alan Buckley and Bernie Wright.

He had another splendidly consistent season in 1976/77, missing only four games. Though he scored only 6 goals all season, three of them came in the 6-1 win against Reading in February, to bring back memories of when Colin Taylor was getting hat-tricks from the wing. Miah also played in two memorable cup ties that season, being on the wrong end of a 4-2 League Cup defeat by his former club, Nottingham Forest, and being one of the eleven who battled bravely in a 1-0 FA Cup defeat by Manchester United at Old Trafford.

He was also in the side that reached the fifth round of the FA Cup and lost 4-1 to Arsenal at Highbury in 1977/78. Then, in what proved to be his last game as a Walsall player, he netted in the 3-1 win over Rotherham at the end of 1977/78. Walsall just missed out on promotion that season but a season later, without Miah's ability to cross accurately with either foot, they were relegated – although there were naturally other factors involved as well.

Miah, meanwhile, had moved on to Bristol Rovers in the summer of 1978 and at Eastville he also had his moments, such as when he got a hat-trick in a 4-1 win over Swansea on Boxing Day 1979.

After leaving Rovers in 1980, Miah had a short spell with Trowbridge Town before moving back to his native town to play for Cork FC.

Johnny Devlin
Striker/midfielder, 1947-1952

	First Team Appearances	Goals
Football League	159	49
FA Cup	7	1
TOTAL	166	50

Older Walsall fans were saddened to hear of the death of Johnny Devlin, early in 2001, as they remembered him as one of the top players in the Walsall sides just after the war: a skilful ball player and tactician and a very useful finisher.

Born in Airdrie in 1917, Johnny had already had considerable experience in Scotland before coming south of the Border. He had been with Hibernian before the war, had played with a number of famous players in Services football during the war and had played regularly for Kilmarnock in 1946/47 and the first part of 1947/48.

Then, in December 1947, Harry Hibbs signed this player who had a reputation of being an outstanding midfielder and could also play up front when required. Johnny had just celebrated his thirtieth birthday, but the hope that he still had some good football in him was well founded.

He scored on his debut, a 3-0 win over Aldershot on Christmas Day, scored again in the return game two days later and missed only one game for the rest of that season. He calmly slotted home penalties against both Notts County and Bristol City and in a thrilling end-of-season 6-0 win at Exeter, he netted twice.

Johnny seemed to love playing against Notts County, who had England striker Tommy Lawton in their side at that time, and he netted two penalties in a 3-2 win over them on a rainy Thursday night in September 1948. Then, the following January, he got the extra-time match-winner at Craven Cottage, as Walsall – from the lower half of the Third Division

(South) – beat Second Division promotion candidates Fulham on their own ground.

Johnny got 12 goals in that first full season, but his greatest scoring feat came in September 1949 when, on another memorable Thursday evening (though it was fine this time), he got five goals in a 7-1 hammering of Torquay. His goal tally that season was 22, playing as an old fashioned inside forward. In addition to his own considerable contributions as a player, he also played a great part in the development of young players such as Jimmy Condie (who had followed him from Scotland) and Phil Chapman.

The 1950/51 season saw him playing increasingly in midfield, but he still released the occasional unstoppable shot, such as the opening goal against Millwall in February 1951 that went in off the bar from thirty yards – the goalkeeper was Malcolm Finlayson, who later went on to give great service to Wolves.

It was in 1952 that Johnny moved on – but not far – to become player-manager of Bloxwich Strollers. He combined this with a job at the old Talbot Stead. He returned to Fellows Park for a spell under Bill Moore, as reserve-team coach in the early 1960s, and lived in Walsall for the rest of his days, always being ready to chat to fans that he met.

One of the things that Johnny is remembered with affection for was his ability not just to score penalties, but to earn them. 'Doing a Devlin' is still an expression used by some older fans. Johnny's skills are etched into the club's history.

Don Dorman

Striker/midfielder, 1954-1957

	First Team Appearances	Goals
Football League	114	34
FA Cup	8	1
TOTAL	122	35

Don Dorman followed in the footsteps of Don Dearson in playing for Birmingham, Coventry and Walsall, in that order. He too gave excellent service to the Saddlers near the end of his career.

Born in Hall Green in 1922, Don played for Shirley Juniors before the war. During the war years, he distinguished himself as a paratrooper at Arnhem, being wounded and captured but surviving to link up with Birmingham City in 1946 and to make his debut for them in the opening game of 1947. Although he only had short spells of first-team football with the Blues, he showed real class in midfield and hammered home the occasional powerful shot, as in the 4-1 win over Leeds on Valentine's Day 1948.

After 64 games and 6 goals for Blues, Don moved to Coventry in September 1951 and, after settling into midfield in his first season, blossomed as a striker in 1952/53, with hat-tricks in successive games against Crystal Palace and Torquay. He went on to get 31 goals in 94 games for Coventry and then moved to Walsall in October 1954, just after the Saddlers had survived three successive re-election applications.

He proved to be one of the very best of Major Buckley's many signings. Although his debut game at Aldershot ended in a 4-0 defeat, he raised the spirits of fans on a wet night the following April by scoring two of the goals in a 6-1 win over Northampton. Whether playing in midfield or up front, Don was an inspirational figure who took over as skipper in due course.

One of his finest hours was in December 1956 when, after being injured in a tough 2-2 draw against his former club at Highfield Road a week earlier, he was declared fit only just before the kick-off of a game against Millwall but went on to get a hat-trick in a 7-0 win and just a week after that got two more goals in a 6-3 win over Norwich. He got 18 goals that season and played for the representative Third Division (South) side in the annual game against the Third Division (North).

What a shock it was for Walsall fans when, at the end of that season, Don announced his retirement in order to become a full-time scout with Birmingham City. Though he was almost thirty-five, he was playing possibly the best football of his career.

As a scout he was even more effective than as a player, however, his discoveries for the Blues (having succeeded Walter Taylor as chief scout) including Trevor Francis. After a quarter of a century back at Blues, he had a spell as chief scout of Aston Villa before retiring from football in 1985. Don Dorman is still talked of by older Walsall fans as the perfect example of the skilled ball player who could also score goals.

Jimmy Dudley

Midfielder, 1959-1964

	First Team Appearances	Goals
Football League	167	3
FA Cup	6	0
FL Cup	3	0
TOTAL	176	3

Jimmy Dudley was another of the players who gave great service to Walsall, despite the fact that they had already celebrated their thirtieth birthdays when they joined the club.

Jimmy was, in fact, thirty-one, having been born in Gartosh Glasgow in 1928. His brother, George Dudley, had played for West Brom before the war and had made a total of 37 guest appearances for Walsall. Jimmy followed George to The Hawthorns and their careers overlapped for a couple of seasons at the end of the war.

Dudley went on to set up what was then a record 166 consecutive appearances for Albion and, in the course of 320 games for them, he gained an FA Cup winners' medal in 1954 and a Scotland 'B' international cap.

He arrived at Fellows Park in December 1959, to strengthen Walsall's squad as they sought promotion from the Fourth Division. He made his debut in a 1-0 win over Aldershot and his first eight games resulted in six wins and two draws. He was equally happy on either the right side or the left side of midfield and played a key part in promotion in successive seasons, to land Walsall back in the Second Divison after a gap of sixty years.

On arrival there, Jimmy immediately looked the part. He played in every game in 1961/62 and missed just eight games in the following sea-

son, when Walsall just failed to avoid relegation. He played on for one more season back in the Third Division and he still looked the part, always calm on the ball and looking to lay on an opening, but ever-ready to drop back into a defensive role when Walsall were under pressure.

After leaving Fellows Park in 1964, he played for a time for Stourbridge and then for Guest Motors, the firm for whom he worked for over thirty years, just a mile from where he had attended Hill Top School as a boy.

In a different era, Jimmy Dudley might well have won a number of full Scottish international caps, for he was, in many ways, the complete midfielder. In addition, he had a splendid temperament. He was not easily provoked in the heat of the game, and one recalls his readiness to help unload the team kit on the occasions when he was 'twelfth man' in those pre-substitute days.

Billy Evans

Striker, 1934-1939

	First Team Appearances	Goals
Football League	115	54
FA Cup	9	7
Others	8	3
TOTAL	132	64

Born in Cannock in 1914, Billy Evans was playing for Cannock Chase Colliery when he was spotted by Walsall. He got his first goal in a Walsall shirt when he netted in a reserve game at Tamworth in September 1934, just a few weeks after manager Bill Slade had signed him.

Billy Evans was a left-winger in those days and it must have been a shock when the manager who had signed him resigned a few weeks into the season. Nothing was going right for the team at that time and new boss Andy Wilson soon gave Billy a first-team chance – in a game at Doncaster in October 1924 – but for some time the team continued to struggle and Billy did not get a regular place until near the end of the season. By that time he had thrilled reserve-team fans with 24 goals in the Birmingham Combination and he came good in the first-team game against Tranmere in February 1935, when he provided a perfect cross from a corner for Bill Sheppard to head home and then scored himself after being put through by Ben Woolhouse.

Early in the following season it seemed that Billy's main role for Walsall would be, in the words of a contemporary report, 'getting the ball from an opponent and putting it at the feet of Gilbert Alsop'. However, when Gilbert was taken ill just before a game against Mansfield in October 1935, Billy was tried as leader of the attack – and he responded with a remarkable five-goal burst in a 7-0 win.

Gilbert was in fact suffering from tonsillitis. On his recovery he was sold to West Bromwich Albion and Billy took over the number nine shirt permanently. He responded so well to the challenge that by the end of the season he had netted 25 goals and in the following season he got another 23. After that, injury made his appearances more sporadic but he kept up the remarkable scoring rate of one every two games.

In the summer of 1939, Billy moved to Tranmere and played in the three League games that took place before the Second World War was declared. He came back to the Midlands, but we have no record of him playing football after that.

Billy's career was a short one, but what a glorious one! He got three hat-tricks, quite apart from the five goals mentioned above, and his football philosophy was delightfully simple – get the ball, beat the man and try for goal or, if that's not possible, give the ball to somebody better placed.

	First Team Appearances	Goals
Football League	231	7
FA Cup	20	1
FL Cup	12	0
TOTAL	263	8

Mick Evans was everybody's idea of a big, stout-hearted defender and he never gave less than a hundred per cent to the team that he served.

Born in West Bromwich in 1964, he played for the Birmingham County FA while still at school. He then played for Vono Sports, before linking up with Walsall in 1963 and turning professional in 1964. He was just nineteen when he made his first-team debut in the home game against Hull City in December 1965, and had something of a baptism of fire as Hull won 4-2 with their strike force of Ken Wagstaff and Bruce Bannister, as they moved towards promotion.

Mick then came back into the team to stay after John Harris's serious injury on the opening day of the 1966/7 season, missing only five games all season and looking as durable as if he had been playing for years. As he gained in confidence, Mick also ventured forward more often and he was an impressive sight as all fourteen stone of him surged down the left flank.

Although he had played as a central defender in his early days, he played almost exclusively in the number three shirt for Walsall, though he was tried as an emergency striker in a goalless draw at Doncaster in February 1970. He also snatched some useful goals, four of them in the 1970/71 season when Walsall battled successfully against a relegation threat.

After well over 250 games, Mick moved to Swansea in December 1972, just after Harry Gregg had taken over as manager. He was just the man then needed by the Swans as they battled for their very existence and he spent two and half seasons there. One of his least happy games, however, was on his return to Fellows Park for an FA Cup tie in November 1974, when a George Andrews effort squeezed past him as he stood on the line, to give Walsall victory.

He had made just over 100 League and cup appearances for the Swans when he followed Harry Gregg to Crewe in the summer of 1975 and missed only six games in his first season there. He played a total of 82 games in two seasons and scored 4 goals. One unusual feature of Mick's career was that, though he played over 400 League and cup games for his three Football League teams, he appeared only twice as substitute. Both these games were while he was with Walsall – at Bristol Rovers in February 1970 and at home to Shrewsbury later the same year.

In 1977, Mick moved into non-League football with Worcester and later played for Stafford Rangers, Rushall Olympic and Halesowen. In more recent times he has played for a number of All Stars teams in charity games.

Roy Faulkner
Striker, 1958-1961

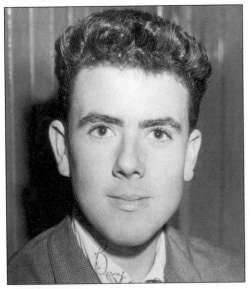

	First Team Appearances	Goals
Football League	100	43
FA Cup	4	0
FL Cup	1	0
TOTAL	105	43

Roy Faulkner had a comparatively short time with Walsall, but during that time he proved himself a quality striker who played a big part in the club's rise from the lower half of the Third Division (South) via the Fourth Division to the Second Division.

Born in Manchester in 1935, Roy graduated via the Manchester City junior ranks. His first-team debut for them was in a First Division game against Birmingham at St Andrews, when he got the final goal in a 4-3 defeat. He also scored against Everton, Blackpool and Sheffield United that season and his record of four goals in just seven days was impressive. However, with players such as Bobby Johnstone, Joe Hayes and the one and only Don Revie blocking his way to a regular first-team place, Roy gave up waiting and moved to Walsall in March 1958.

He again scored on his debut, this time the opening goal in a 3-2 win at Swindon, and he followed this up with two goals in his first home game, a 3-0 win over Port Vale. Though there was nothing at stake at that stage of the season, with Walsall certain to figure in the new Fourth Division after the close-season restructuring, he had already shown that he had much to offer for a side who so needed support for ace goalscorer Tony Richards up front.

Roy made a quiet start to the following season, not achieving a regular place immediately but, after netting the opening goal in a 3-2 win at the beginning of October, he did not look back. He got two goals in each of two successive home wins – 5-1 against Southport and 6-0 against Crewe – and ended the season with 13 goals in 28 games as Walsall just missed promotion on account of that indifferent start to the season.

There was no slip-up in 1959/60, however. Roy scored in each of the first five games as Walsall dropped only one point and romped to the top of the table, where they stayed. Roy matched Tony Richards almost goal for goal as they got 21 and 24 respectively.

Roy lost just a little of his edge after a bright start to the 1960/61 season and Tommy Wilson arrived from Nottingham Forest to partner Tony Richards for much of what was another promotion season. Faulkner did make a couple more appearances before the end of that campaign, however, and in his last home game, he opened the scoring in a 4-1 win over Bristol City.

He left Walsall in the summer of 1960 and became successful outside the game as a company rep., but fans who saw him in those glorious promotion days will easily remember his finishing power, with netting from a tight angle his speciality.

Graeme Forbes

Central defender, 1986-1990

	First Team Appearances	Goals
Football League	173	9
FA Cup	13	1
FL Cup	12	2
Others	16	2
TOTAL	214	14

This tall craggy defender, who gave nothing away in defence and was a considerable threat to any defence when he moved upfield, was possibly Tommy Coakley's finest signing, as he fine-tuned the side that he inherited in 1986 to produce the promotion team of 1988.

Born in Forfar in 1958, Graeme played for Lochee United before joining Motherwell in 1980. He played regularly for them in the Scottish First Division for over six seasons, before moving to Walsall in September 1986, making his debut in a 3-1 home defeat by Doncaster. In his next two games he was on the wrong end of 5-1 and 4-1 defeats by Wigan and Port Vale respectively, but soon he was commanding the centre of the Walsall defence alongside Peter Hart.

He also moved upfield to good effect and by the end of the season he had scored four goals, including a last-minute winner against Torquay in the Freight Rover Trophy in December. His best season was, however, 1987/88, as he played a total of 59 games and netted five goals as Walsall won promotion to the old Second Division after a replayed play-off final.

He then missed only one game in 1988/89, as he skippered a side that just couldn't hold on to their Second Division place, and

1989/90 was another tough season in which Graeme battled throughout, missed only three games and played in the last-ever League match at Fellows Park. Even so, it was relegation again at the end. Graeme moved back north of the Border before Bescot was opened. He had a short spell with Dundee, while Walsall fans reflected on his time with the club, which had seen it promoted once and relegated twice.

Powerful and consistent, Graeme was one of many Scots who have made their mark with Walsall over the years. He both gave and took some hard knocks, and it was his misfortune that, after helping Walsall into the Second Division, the club's financial situation deteriorated to the extent that it did not have the resources to build a successful Second Division team around him.

Reg Foulkes

Central defender and striker, 1945-1950

	First Team Appearances	Goals
Football League	160	6
FA Cup	15	0
TOTAL	175	6

Reg Foulkes was one member of what many older fans consider to be the best half-back line in Walsall's history, and the names Crutchley, Foulkes and Newman readily occur when the 1940s are being discussed.

Born in Shrewsbury in 1923, he was an England schoolboy international before the war and was on Birmingham's books during the war years. He was then signed by Harry Hibbs, who had known him at Birmingham, soon after the latter took over as manager of Walsall in 1945.

Reg's first game in a Walsall shirt was in a wartime game at Norwich in November 1945, as he just happened to line up with Ron Crutchley and 'Nutty' Newman either side of him. This combination was a key element of the side from then on and they went on to reach the final of the Third Division (South) Cup, which was played in that intermediate season just before the normal Football League resumed.

Foulkes was thus the natural choice at the heart of the defence in the Third Division (South) in the seasons immediately after the war. Cool and calm, a scrupulously fair tackler and powerful in the air, he had some splendid games against Notts County, whose key striker was England international Tommy Lawton.

Even when injured in a game at Ipswich in January 1947, Reg scored a goal while hobbling in the forward line (there were no substitutes in those days) and he missed only two games in the first three seasons after the war. He succeeded 'Nutty' Newman as captain in 1948 and then in 1949/50, when Walsall were struggling to score goals, he played up front and scored twice in three games.

In 1950 he moved to Norwich. He immediately became captain and in three successive seasons they finished second, third and fourth in the Third Division (South) and played in a thrilling 2-1 FA Cup win against Arsenal at Highbury in January 1954, when former Walsall team-mate Doug Lishman was in the Arsenal side.

After 238 games for Norwich, he moved to Wisbech as player-manager in 1956, then went on to Kings Lynn. He was back at Norwich looking after the reserves in the early 1960s and then, after qualifying as an accountant, returned to the Midlands and worked for Star Aluminium in Wolverhampton for many years. As the twenty-first century arrived, Reg was with his hometown club Shrewsbury and working as an accountant, still as cool and calm as in his great days as a central defender.

	First Team Appearances	Goals
Football League	180	8
FA Cup	8	0
TOTAL	188	8

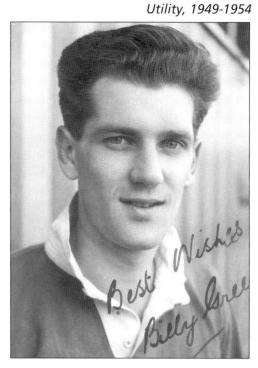

Billy Green was possibly the most versatile player ever to play for Walsall and it was most unfortunate that his splendidly consistent service to the club came at one of the low spells in the club's history.

Born in Hull in 1927, Billy linked up with Wolves during the war years and played three first-team games for them during that time. He then featured mainly in their third team, until linking up with Walsall in September 1949, joining a long line of players to move from Molineux to Fellows Park in those days. Walsall had just changed from claret and blue to red shirts and Bill's first appearance in one was in a 1-1 draw at Bristol Rovers in mid-October. He also played in a number of games up front before the end of that season.

In 1950/51 he ended the season on the left flank of the defence and in 1951/52 he played in every game and made a remarkable appearance in goal at Southend on Boxing Day, after regular goalkeeper Jackie Lewis had been injured 24 hours earlier. Bill was Man of the Match, despite Walsall's 3-0 defeat and he also looked the part later in the season when playing at the heart of the defence.

In 1952/53 Walsall used twenty-seven different players and in 1953/54 they used thirty-three, yet Bill was ever-present in both seasons' line-ups. Amongst his most memorable games was the one against Brighton on Easter Tuesday 1953, when he played up front and got the third goal in a 3-0 win over Brighton as Walsall welcomed new manager Major Frank Buckley with one of their best performances of the season. Then, in January 1954, he played heroically in the twice-replayed FA Cup tie against Lincoln, but had the bad luck to concede a penalty and an own goal after Walsall had taken the lead.

In the summer of 1954 he moved to Wrexham. He played in an FA Cup tie against his old club, which the Saddlers won 2-1 in November 1954. Over 16,000 saw that game and there were more than twice as many as that just over two years later when Manchester United won 5-0 in another memorable game. 1957 saw him back in the Midlands with Telford United and then, after spells with Caernarfon and Pwllhelli, he retired in 1960. Walsall fans were pleased to receive a greeting from Bill in 1996, only to be saddened a few weeks later to hear of his death. He had been a tireless battler in the cause of Walsall Football Club.

Ron Green
Goalkeeper, 1979-1985 & 1989-1991

	First Team Appearances	Goals
Football League	230	0
FA Cup	15	0
FL Cup	13	0
Others	7	0
TOTAL	265	0

Ron Green is one of a number of players to have had separate spells with Walsall in a playing career that stretched over a quarter of a century. He was in the Walsall goal in some of the most memorable games in the club's history.

Born in Birmingham in 1956, Ron played for Alvechurch for two seasons before linking up with Walsall and making his debut in a 3-0 defeat at Rotherham in October 1977. Mick Kearns was the first-choice goalkeeper at that time and after Ian Turner's arrival from Southampton in January 1979, Ron was third choice for a while. He was brought back for the last game of 1978/79, which again happened to be at Rotherham. Walsall were already booked for relegation and Ron found himself on the wrong end of a 4-1 defeat.

1979/80 was, however, a different story. Mick Kearns had by this time moved on to Wolves and, a month into the new season, Ron took over from Ian Turner and played in a total of 43 League and cup games as Walsall climbed straight back out of the Fourth Division. A mystery infection kept him out of the side for the first three months of the following season, as Neil Freeman and Martin Conneally, as well as Ian Turner, had spells in goal, but Ron was back for the last 24 games. In the very last one he made a penalty save late in the game at Bramall Lane, to keep Walsall up and send Sheffield United down to the bottom division.

Ron was an ever-present in 1981/82, then was injured on 1 April 1983 and for a time battled with Mick Kearns (back again from Wolves) and Tony Godden for the first-team spot – but Ron was in goal for the quarter-final Milk Cup win at Rotherham (a happier visit than on his first two visits there) and that remarkable 2-2 semi-final draw at Liverpool.

Soon afterwards, Ron was loaned to West Brom and in the summer of 1984 he moved to Shrewsbury. From there he moved to Bristol Rovers on loan in the following March and kept five successive clean sheets. He joined Rovers permanently in the summer of 1985 and then a season later began two seasons with Scunthorpe. In August 1988 he had his first sample of the top flight with Wimbledon, but was loaned soon afterwards to Shrewsbury. Then, in August 1989, he returned to Walsall at the age of thirty-three.

He was first choice in the first season at Bescot in 1990/91 before joining Kidderminster (then in the Conference) in August 1991. He was briefly back in League football in 1992/93 when he played 4 games for Colchester, who were then managed by former Walsall team-mate, Roy McDonough. Since then he has had three spells with Bromsgove and one each with Happy Valley (Hong Kong), Hereford, Moor Green, Oldbury, and Boldmere, finally hanging up his boots in the year 2000.

Cool under pressure, Ron was a splendidly consistent, if unspectacular, goalkeeper. Despite playing for countless other clubs with distinction, his greatest days were those he spent with Walsall.

Frank Gregg
Defender, 1960-1972

	First Team Appearances	Goals
Football League	393	3
FA Cup	30	0
FL Cup	21	1
TOTAL	444	4

Frank Gregg is a typical example of what was a key feature of Walsall teams of the 1960s, 1970s and 1980s, being a home-grown player discovered by Ron Jukes and remaining a one-club man as far as League football was concerned.

Born in Stourbridge in 1942, Frank played for Brierley Hill Schools and Birmingham County Boys before joining the Walsall ground staff and signing as a professional in October 1959. Reserve-team followers (and there were a fair number of them in those days) were already talking of 'this lad, Gregg' before Frank made his first-team debut in a Third Division game at Reading in October 1960. That turned out to be Walsall's second successive promotion season, but Frank's next first-team games were the following season, in the Second Division. He played fairly regularly in 1962/63 as he competed for one of the two full-back spots with Granville Palin and John Sharples but, sadly, it turned out to be a relegation campaign.

It was clear, however, that Frank (still not quite twenty-one) would be one of the players around whom the new Walsall would be built, and by 1964/65 he had the distinction of playing in every game, as chairman Bill Harrison and manager Ray Shaw put together a side that was destined to achieve some memorable cup results but miss out on promotion, which at one stage had seemed to be only a matter of time.

Frank had another excellent season in 1965/66. In addition to defensive duties, he got a late equalizer against QPR in a League Cup tie that ultimately earned Walsall a share of a 41,000 gate in the next round at The Hawthorns. In 1966/67, he again showed his versatility by netting penalties in successive games against Oldham and Swindon, and then in 1967/68 he played in all 54 League and cup games, including the FA Cup win at Crystal Palace and the two FA Cup ties against Liverpool.

Frank maintained his consistent form until the end of 1973, when he moved to Burton Albion and for a time played again in front of Bob Wesson, who had been the Walsall goalkeeper in many of Frank's games for the club.

Frank has attended a number of players' reunions in recent years, and is always happy to talk modestly about his playing days when fans saw him as the ideal modern flank defender – equally happy on either side of the field, firm and fair in the tackle and one of Walsall's first overlapping defenders.

Teddy Groves
Utility, 1921-1930

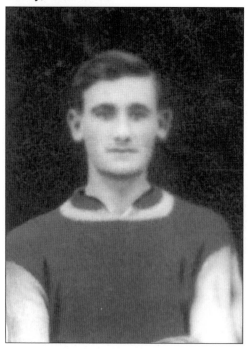

	First Team Appearances	Goals
Football League	243	25
FA Cup	13	2
TOTAL	256	27

Although he was no relation to Albert Groves, the former Wolves stalwart who managed Walsall for a short spell, Teddy Groves came to the club towards the end of Albert's time, so that both Groves, A. and Groves, E. appeared on the team sheet and confused some of the less discerning fans.

Born in Walsall in 1900, Teddy, who had previously played for Talbot Stead Works team, made his first-team debut on the right flank of the defence in a 2-0 win at Crewe in April 1922, near the end of the first season in the Third Division (North). Teddy's next game was in the following season, when he was in midfield on an unhappy day at Chesterfield when the home side won 6-0.

Happier times followed, however, as Teddy was the man to succeed George Reid up front after the latter's move to Cardiff in December 1922. In only his second game in the number nine shirt, he netted in a 2-0 win at Lincoln and by the end of the season his tally was 13 goals in 23 games. Over the next two seasons he played steadily up front and also did well when he filled temporary gaps in the defence caused by injuries to left-back George Smith

and central defender Sid Bowser. Then, after the transfer of right-flank defender Walter Webster to Scunthorpe in 1925, Teddy took over the number two shirt and was virtually ever-present over the next two seasons. In 1927/28 he played mainly in midfield as David Fairhurst took over the right-back spot but, after David's move to Newcastle early in 1929, Teddy was back for a time in defence.

He was unlucky to miss playing in the 1930 FA Cup tie at Villa Park, when Fred Walters was at right-back, but he played a few more games after that before ending almost ten years at Walsall in 1930. He played for a time for Shrewsbury, Wellington and Hednesford after leaving the club. He then worked for many years at Deritend Stamping, Wednesbury, in the dyeing shop. It seemed somehow appropriate that Teddy, who had so readily changed positions in his footballing days, should be an expert in sorting out the different colours of products in later years.

Stockily-built, he was one of the players whom those who saw him play still talked of twenty or more years later.

	First Team Appearances	Goals
Football League	198	0
FA Cup	10	0
FL Cup	2	0
TOTAL	210	0

Bill Guttridge was one of the gamest defenders to have worn the Saddlers' colours and, although he had the nickname 'Chopper', he was always a firm and fair tackler rather than a hatchet man.

Born in Darlaston in 1931, Bill played for Metroshaft Works before joining Wolves, initially as an amateur, in 1947. He played just seven first-team games in his seven seasons with them when there was a vast array of defensive talent available. The first of them was a memorable 3-3 draw at Villa Park on Christmas Day, 1951. He moved to Walsall in November 1954, when Major Frank Buckley was manager, and proved to be one of the old Major's best signings.

Walsall were on their way to a fourth successive re-election application when Bill made his first-team debut against Newport in November 1954, and the game ended 3-3 as it had in his Wolves debut. Within a few weeks he was playing in an FA Cup-tie against Chelsea at Stamford Bridge, and though Walsall lost 2-0, there was a gate of over 40,000 and the Chelsea team gained a healthy respect for Bill's tackling.

Bill lost his place for a time to Harry Haddington in 1955/56, but returned to the side to play some useful games in midfield and at the heart of the defence. He then took over the left-back spot in 1957/58 after an injury to Eric Perkins and he partnered Harry Haddington for most of the Fourth Division championship season of 1959/60.

Guttridge competed with Granville Palin and John Sharples for the two flank defensive spots in the 1960/61 season after Harry Haddington's serious injury, before being sidelined by a cartilage operation. Then, in the early days back in the Second Division in 1961/62, he played heroically in a 3-2 win at Preston, where he twice cleared off the line, being laid out by the power of the shot on one occasion. He suffered a badly-bruised eye after a collision with Sunderland's Stan Anderson later in the season, but still battled on in another game that season.

After leaving Walsall in 1962, Bill had two good seasons with Macclesfield, being voted Player of the Season in one of them. He then moved on to Stourbridge, before ending his career in 1967/68 as player-manager of his native Darlaston.

Many Walsall fans still talk about Bill and recall with affection his return to Fellows Park for Albert McPherson's benefit in 1964, when he scored a tremendous goal from thirty yards into the Laundry End net.

Bill is always a popular visitor to functions at Bescot, for few players before or since have been more universally popular. Older fans still remember Bill's famous sliding tackles with affection.

Harry Haddington
Defender, 1955-1960

	First Team Appearances	Goals
Football League	226	0
FA Cup	9	0
TOTAL	237	0

Harry Haddington was an outstanding defender and captain, who led Walsall to promotion from the Fourth Division in 1959/60 and had set them on the way to going up again a season later, when a broken leg cruelly ended his Football League career.

Born in Scarborough in 1931, Harry played for a Scarborough junior team before linking up with former Football League club Bradford Park Avenue in 1949. He played in just two Football League games for them, against Chesterfield and Scunthorpe in the old Third Division (North) in 1951/52. He then moved to West Brom, together with striker Derek Kevan, in the summer of 1953.

He did not break through into the first team at The Hawthorns, as Stan Rickaby held down the right flank of the defence spot, and so it was in search of first-team football that Harry moved to Walsall in the summer of 1955. He made his debut in the number six shirt in a 3-2 defeat at Torquay at the end of August, and then a few weeks later settled into the right-back slot. He was partnered first by Albert Vinall, then by Eric Perkins and finally by Bill Guttridge, and he was rarely out of the team

for the next five years. He was an ever-present in both 1957/58 and in the 1959/60 Fourth Division championship season, by which time he was captaining the side. He saw Walsall off to an explosive start with three wins and a draw in their first four games back in the Third Division, but then came disaster. Early in the game against Tranmere, near the end of September, he was carried off with a broken leg. The spirit that he fostered in the Walsall team carried the ten men (those were pre-substitute days) to a 3-1 win, but Harry was never fit for League football again.

He struggled on for two seasons with Worcester City and then retired. Happily, even without him, Walsall battled to promotion as Granville Palin moved to the number two spot and Albert McPherson took over as captain.

Harry Haddington was the model professional, a great all-round defender and an inspirational captain.

Johnny Hancocks

Winger, 1938-1946

	First Team Appearances	Goals
Football League	30	9
FA Cup	8	1
Others	1	0
TOTAL	39	10

Johnny Hancocks was one of the smallest wingers ever to wear a Walsall shirt, or any other shirt for that matter, but no-one packed a more powerful shot.

Born in Oakengates in 1919, Johnny played for Oakengates Town before moving to Walsall in 1938. He made his first-team debut in a 2-2 draw against Aldershot in October 1938 and scored his first goal on Boxing Day of that year. He was only nineteen at the time, but was entrusted with a penalty and duly banged it home. In fact, five of his nine goals that season were from the penalty spot and he also provided crosses for a fair proportion of the 23 that Gilbert Alsop scored.

Johnny was very active during the war years, working as an army PT instructor, playing for Walsall whenever he could and on other occasions guesting for Chester, Crewe, Nottingham Forest and Wrexham. All in all, he scored 35 goals in 94 games for Walsall during the war and he ended his Walsall career by starring in their run to the Third Division (South) Cup final in 1938/39, when they lost 1-0 to Bournemouth at Stamford Bridge.

Just a week after that game, Johnny moved to Wolves for just £5,000 – and what a bargain they got. In their first post-war game, he netted in a 6-1 win over Arsenal and he went on to score 168 goals in 378 games for them and

also won three full England caps. After leaving Wolves in 1957, Johnny had a spell as player-manager of Wellington Town and later assisted Cambridge United in their pre-League days, before moving on to Oswestry and GKN Sankey. Until his retirement in 1979, he worked for the Oakengates Ironfounders, John Maddock.

Sadly, Johnny died in 1994 after a stroke. Although he had his best days with Wolves, he still rates as the finest winger Walsall have ever fielded. The power of his shooting with just size three boots had to be seen to be believed. So did his crossing from either wing after the ball had seemed certain to run out of play. He won both an FA Cup and a Football League Championship medal with Wolves and starred in the remarkable wins over Spartak and Honved in 1954 that thrilled the whole nation. He brought great pleasure to fans in the dark days of the war and the euphoric post-war era.

Johnny Hancocks releases a typical power drive from his size three boots.

	First Team Appearances	Goals
Football League	74	2
FA Cup	7	0
FL Cup	4	0
TOTAL	85	2

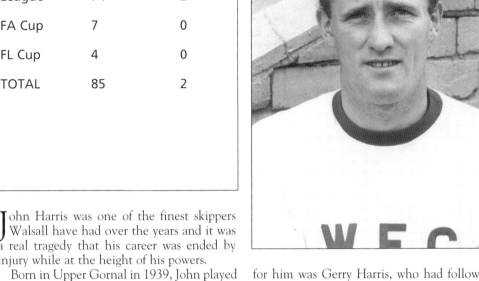

John Harris was one of the finest skippers Walsall have had over the years and it was a real tragedy that his career was ended by injury while at the height of his powers.

Born in Upper Gornal in 1939, John played for Sedgley Rovers before joining Wolves as a junior and turning professional in 1958. He made his first-team debut in a 3-2 win over West Ham in August 1961, but just two days later had the cruel luck to break a leg in 2-2 draw against Aston Villa. He battled back to play one more game for Wolves (a 3-3 draw at Manchester City in the following season) and with so much defensive talent at Molineux at the time (including namesake Gerry Harris), John moved to Walsall in January 1965 as part of a major rebuilding programme after Bill Harrison had taken over as chairman and Ray Shaw had moved in as manager.

He made his debut in a 1-1 draw against Shrewsbury, held his place for the rest of that season and was appointed captain for 1965/66. He had an outstanding season, leading his side to a tremendous display at West Brom in the League Cup, that ultimately ended in defeat, and to a magnificent 2-0 victory at Stoke in the FA Cup, when Walsall played most of the game with ten men after Jimmy McMorran had been seriously injured. John missed only one game that season and the man who deputized

for him was Gerry Harris, who had followed him from Wolves.

Then, in the opening game of 1966/67, John suffered a serious knee injury in a game against Mansfield and was never fully fit again, though he did battle back gamely to play a few games. There was real drama at Oldham in March 1967, when Nick Atthey was injured in a pre-match kick-in and John, who had travelled with the team, took over at a moment's notice and played a fine game in a 3-0 win.

He had an eight-match spell back in the team again in October and November 1968, but he was still troubled by his knee and after a short spell as reserve-team coach he retired from the game and went into the building trade. John was a typical man of Gornal, with a broad Black Country accent and splendid sense of humour that lit up the dressing room and the team coach. Splendidly calm under pressure, he was an inspiration to all around him, both on and off the field. Older fans will readily remember the calm way he netted two penalties in a game at Shrewsbury in March 1966.

Colin Harrison

Utility, 1963-1981

	First Team Appearances	Goals
Football League	473	33
FA Cup	37	0
FL Cup	19	1
TOTAL	529	34

Colin Harrison holds the record for the most first-team appearances in the history of Walsall Football Club, having played 530 times for his one and only League club.

Born in Pelsall in 1946, he was recruited by chief scout Ron Jukes, who still remembers the dog that barred his entry when he visited Colin's house in quest of his signature. Fortunately, Ron succeeded in getting it, and Colin graduated via the junior ranks to sign professionally in 1963. He made his first-team debut in September 1964, when he appeared on the left wing in a goal-less draw at Southend. He was in and out of the team over the next two seasons and at different times played in midfield, defence and attack. He netted his first goal while playing up front in a 3-0 win over Reading in October 1965.

Colin's versatility made him a popular choice for the number twelve shirt in the early days of substitutes, when teams could only use their substitute to replace an injured player. Eventually, Colin settled into the number three shirt in the 1969/70 season, and at this stage he had developed his power shooting that brought him two spectacular goals against Southport in August 1969.

For the next few seasons he fluctuated between defence and midfield. He was an ever-present in 1972/73 and in 1974/75 played on the left flank of the defence in the FA Cup win over Manchester United and on the right flank in the win over Newcastle. Then, in the fifth round FA Cup tie at Highbury in February 1978, he played in midfield. Although Walsall lost 4-1, Colin's run early in the game that took him almost half the length of the field is still remembered with affection.

As the 1970s gave way to the 1980s, Colin became reserve-team coach, and amongst his experiences in that role were the scoring of his first hat-trick and a game in goal. However, he was recalled for first-team service again in 1980/81, and he played his last first-team game in a 1-1 draw against Chesterfield in September 1981.

Fans were disappointed when Colin was not retained in a behind-the-scenes role after that, but continued to follow his progress as he had a useful spell with Rushall Olympic, while going into the carpet business at Rugeley.

Colin was one of those players who never had a bad game, whatever position he played in, and he was the perfect example of the local boy made good.

Colin Harrison (extreme left) celebrates in the dressing room after the fourth round FA Cup win over Leicester City in January 1978. Celebrating with him are: Dave Serella, Alun Evans, Mick Bates, Brian Caswell and Alan Birch.

Peter Hart
Midfielder/defender, 1980-1990

	First Team Appearances	Goals
Football League	390	12
FA Cup	28	0
FL Cup	35	0
Others	21	1
TOTAL	474	13

Peter Hart skippered both Huddersfield Town and Walsall to promotion before becoming a clergyman, and at the beginning of the twenty-first century he was vicar of St Martin's Church in the Gillity area of Walsall.

Born in Mexborough in 1957, Peter was still an apprentice when making his first-team debut for Huddersfield against Southend in March 1974, aged just 16 years and 7 months. He captained the Huddersfield side that reached the FA Youth Cup final three months later and, after being in and out of the team and occupying various defensive and midfield positions over the next two seasons, he had a long spell on the right flank of the defence in 1976/77. He had settled into midfield and was captaining the side by the time he led the Terriers to the Fourth Division championship in 1979/80, with Walsall in second place.

At Huddersfield, Peter had played in the same side as Steve Baines, and both met up again at Walsall in 1980 after Peter had moved for a £70,000 fee. Initially, Peter played in midfield, but he was far more impressive after moving into a defensive role. He missed only one game in each of his first four seasons at Fellows Park and skippered the side to that remarkable run to the Milk Cup semi-final in 1983/84.

Few players in Walsall's history have shown the consistency that Peter did throughout the whole of the 1980s, and he skippered the side throughout that protracted 1987/88 season, that ended in triumph with a 4-0 win over Bristol City in a play-off final replay at the end of May.

Back in the Second Division, Peter lost his place after a traumatic 7-0 home defeat by Chelsea in February, but came back to play a few games in 1989/90 – the last season at Fellows Park. In fact the last game to be played at the old stadium was Peter's benefit match against West Brom in May 1990.

Peter has since become a popular preacher of the Gospel, specializing in addresses to young people, in which he uses his football background to good effect. A number of his parishioners remember him from his playing days, when his seemingly relaxed attitute on the field belied an iron determination, a firmness in the tackle and a powerful shot at a time when Walsall experienced more than their share of extreme highs and lows.

	First Team Appearances	Goals
Football League	131	1
FA Cup	7	0
FL Cup	4	0
TOTAL	142	1

Ken Hill was another of the local lads who have made good for Walsall over the years. He gave some outstanding displays in those happy days of the early 1960s, with promotion in successive seasons.

Born in Walsall in 1938, he played as a defender for Walsall Boys and then, while playing for Bescot United and working on the railway, he moved into midfield. By the time he joined Walsall as a professional in November 1956, he was equipped for either role, and, in fact, it was on the right side of the defence that he made his first-team debut in February 1959, in a Fourth Division game against Hartlepool.

He came back into the side in midfield towards the end of the Fourth Division Championship season of 1959/60 and gained a regular place in 1960/61. In that Third Division promotion season, he played like someone who had been in the team for years, and then played in every game in the Second Division in 1961/62. Particularly memorable were the two games against Stoke. In the one at the Victoria Ground he had a powerful long shot well saved, but in the game at Fellows Park he scored with an equally spectacular effort. He also found himself playing against the one and only Stanley Matthews, who commended his performance at the end of the game.

Ken played throughout the brave but vain battle against relegation in 1962/63, when the desperately severe winter caused a mid-season break of almost three months and Walsall took some time to get into their stride when the games were resumed.

In the summer of 1963, he joined Norwich for £17,000. He won many friends amongst the Canaries' fans by dint of his industrious approach to the game and his consistency. In just over two seasons, he played 50 first-team games and 40 reserve games, before returning to Walsall in October 1966. He played nine games in midfield and six in defence before moving into non-League football at the end of that season, playing first for Nuneaton Borough and later for Stourbridge.

Ken has continued to live in the Coalpool area of Walsall and has been a popular visitor to reunions at Bescot at the start of the twenty-first century.

Ken Hodgkisson
Inside forward, 1955-1966

	First Team Appearances	Goals
Football League	336	55
FA Cup	11	1
FL Cup	5	0
TOTAL	356	56

Ken Hodgkisson was one of the most skilful players Walsall have ever fielded, sometimes thinking so far ahead that his potential killer pass was not always capitalized upon by his teammates. He also bagged over 50 goals himself.

Born in West Bromwich in 1933, Ken joined West Brom in 1949, signing as a professional in 1950 and making his first-team debut in a local derby at Villa Park in April 1953. The game ended 1-1, with Ronnie Allen getting Albion's goal in front of nearly 50,000 fans. Ken himself scored in a 2-2 draw at Manchester United's Old Trafford less than a fortnight later, when just over 30,000 were present. He went on to get 4 goals in 21 games, before moving to Walsall in December 1955, soon after Jack Love had taken over as manager.

The reported fee was £1,600 and money has never been better spent, as he was to control the Walsall midfield for the next decade. His debut was undistinguished – a 2-0 defeat at Newport on the last day of 1955 – but soon he was to score the goal that earned a point at Exeter and was fitting in to provide the ammunition for flying winger Fred Morris and prolific striker Tony Richards.

Ken went from strength to strength with his skill on the ball and in both the two seasons in the Fourth Division – 1958, 1959 and 1960 – he also netted double figures himself. He was a star turn again in 1960/61, as Walsall went up for the second season in succession. He has never played better than in those early days back in the Second Division, in the autumn of 1961 when, for a few weeks, Walsall looked capable of going up to the old Fourth Division.

He netted spectacular goals in the away wins at Derby and Preston and, indeed, it was one of his characteristics that the goals he scored were usually quality ones. There were rumours of him wanting to move in the summer of 1962, and young fans ran round with 'Hodgy must stay' banners. Stay he did, and early in 1962/63 he netted a fine inswinging corner against Preston.

He played in every game that season, but could not prevent Walsall going down. He was not quite as regular in the next two seasons back in the Third Division, but early in 1965/66, the first season of substitutes, he got his name in the Walsall record book by becoming the club's first-ever substitute, going on in place of Nick Atthey in a 1-1 draw against Workington. His last game was at Peterborough in September 1965.

Ken moved to Worcester City in the following summer, and then had one season as a player and three as manager of Dudley Town. He was back on the West Brom coaching staff between 1975 and 1985, and for many years appeared in 'All Star' charity games.

Just occasionally, 'Hodgy' was caught in possession and had the crowd howling, but in general his skill on the ball and powerful shooting were a delight. He was the perfect example of the old-fashioned inside forward – a schemer who could score goals.

Sammy Holmes
Midfield/striker, 1888-1902

	First Team Appearances	Goals
Football League	206	30
FA Cup	43	22
TOTAL	249	52

Sammy was one of the real stalwarts of the early days of Walsall Football Club. While it is certain that no one reading this can possibly have seen him play, there are many who wish that they had.

Born in Walsall in 1870, Sammy and his brother, Charlie, both played for Walsall Swifts before the amalgamation of the two Walsall clubs to become the Town Swifts of 1888. Then, when the newly formed team played in the Midland Association in 1888, Sammy gave them the best possible start with four goals in an opening day 6-1 win over Derby St Lukes.

By the time Walsall were elected to the Football League Second Division in 1892, Sammy had scored 49 goals, 7 of them in FA Cup-ties and he wore the number eight shirt in the opening Football League game, a 2-1 defeat by Darwen. He missed only the occasional game in the next nine seasons, and was an ever-present in 1894/95 and 1900/01. Amongst his outstanding feats was a hat-trick in a 3-1 FA Cup win at Stourbridge in November 1893. Just as he had played in the first Walsall Football League game, he played in the last one before they lost their place (fortunately just temporarily) in 1901.

This game was against Middlesbrough and ended 0-0, with Sammy playing in midfield.

This had become his more regular position in those days, though he played back up front again in the following season on a number of occasions. Sammy scored FA Cup goals against Brierley Hill and New Brompton, to earn a prestigious game against Bury that attracted nearly 10,000 fans to the West Bromwich Road ground, only for Walsall to lose 5-0 on a snowbound pitch.

Holmes then played just one more game for Walsall (a week later at Whitwick) before a bad knee injury put him out of first-team football, though he did play a few reserve games and a few games for Dudley Town after that.

Sammy still holds the record for the most FA Cup appearances (43) and also the most FA Cup goals (22) in the history of Walsall Football Club. He was relatively small of stature, but he had a great heart, a first-class engine and an eye for goal. He set the standard that the best Walsall players have maintained over the years.

SEASON 1893-4 SECOND DIVISION

WEST BROMWICH ROAD GROUND — BAILEY — T. HAWKINS — R. SMELLIE — NOV:11TH WALSALL v LIVERPOOL — (COX) — (BRADS...

— DAVIES — R. COOK — N. FORSYTH

S. HOLMES — McWHINNIE — D. COPELAND — S. COX — J. O'BRIEN

Sammy Holmes (extreme left, front row), is seen here as a member of the Walsall team which gave Liverpool a fair old game in what was only Walsall's second-ever season in the Football League. This is one of the few surviving photographs taken on the West Bromwich Road ground, where Walsall played from 1893 to 1896 and in 1900/01. It is interesting that the team lined up for the photograph in the 1-2-3-5 formation in which they played.

Roy John

Goalkeeper, 1928-1932

	First Team Appearances	Goals
Football League	88	0
FA Cup	5	0
TOTAL	93	0

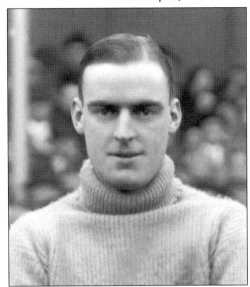

Roy John was quite the most remarkable of the many goalkeepers who have served Walsall with distinction over the years, for he was signed as a full-back, was tried as a goalkeeper in an emergency, and was actually capped by Wales in that position before moving on to win 13 more caps with other clubs.

Born in Neath in 1911, Roy (whose real names were William Ronald) spent the 1927/28 season with Swansea, playing in both defence and midfield. He moved to Walsall in the summer of 1928 and made his first-team debut in a 5-1 defeat at Fulham early in October. He made three more appearances near the end of that season but was playing regularly in the reserves in 1929/30.

At this point something of a goalkeeping crisis arose, after Fred Biddlestone was sold to Aston Villa just after playing against them in the FA Cup. Harry Wait was not getting any younger and though he went back into the first team after Fred's departure, both the two young goalkeepers, Lewis and Cross, were unfit for the reserve game at Oakengates near the end of February 1930. Roy John was pressed into service, and did so well in a goal-less draw that a fortnight later that he was selected for the first-team game against Watford. That game was lost 2-1 and Harry Wait came back for the next three games, but Roy John then made the position his own when he was tried again. In fact, he kept four clean sheets in eight games up to the end of that season.

He missed only three more games in the next two seasons before joining Stoke in April 1932. By that time he had been capped by Wales against Northern Ireland. He went on to win 9 more caps with the Potters, another 3 while with Sheffield United between 1934 and 1936, and a final cap while back at Swansea in 1938/39. In between times, he had also had a short spell with Preston in 1934 and with Manchester United and Newport in 1936/37.

During the war Roy guested for Southport, Blackburn, Burnley and Bolton and played in one wartime international for Wales. At this stage he became a hotel manager, and later kept a public house in Swansea, which unfortunately was bombed. He then took a job with British Steel.

Fans were sorry to hear of his death, aged just sixty-two, in 1973. Roy had been a colourful character, a fine if adventurous goalkeeper with splendid anticipation, and a great crowd-pleaser. One wonders just how many more potential goalkeepers spend their whole careers as outfield players because no emergency cropped up to put them between the sticks.

Stan Jones

Defender, 1957-1960 and 1968-1973

	First Team Appearances	Goals
Football League	236	7
FA Cup	21	0
FL Cup	8	0
TOTAL	265	7

Stan Jones was an outstanding defender who had successful spells with Walsall both at the beginning and near the end of his career.

Born in Highley in 1938, he played for Staffordshire Youths before linking up with Walsall and turning professional in 1956. He made his first-team debut at the heart of the defence in a 2-1 win over Norwich in October 1957. He pressed Albert McPherson hard for his place over the next two years, and had played 32 games (including two as emergency right-back in March 1959) before joining West Brom together with wing-half Peter Billingham in the summer of 1960. He succeeded Joe Kennedy as Albion's number five and was first choice for several seasons, though he was unlucky to miss the 1966 League Cup final through injury.

He was never quite as mobile after that injury and was left out of the side for the League Cup final against QPR in 1967. He returned to Walsall just before the transfer deadline in March 1968, after playing 267 games for Albion. His first game back ended in a 2-1 win over Bristol Rovers, but a few weeks later he conceded an own goal in a 2-1 defeat at Bury after a misunderstanding with goalkeeper Bob Wesson, bringing back memories of an unhappy spell with Albion in which he conceded three own goals in five games.

He got off to an excellent start in 1968/69 by heading the match-winner in the opening game at Shrewsbury and he missed only one game all that season. He missed just six games in the following season, was an ever-present again in 1970/71 and missed just four games in 1971/72, playing in a memorable 2-1 FA Cup defeat by Everton in front of a 45,000 gate at Goodison Park.

He left Walsall for a second time in 1973, and played briefly for Burton Albion. He then had a season as player-manager of Kidderminster, a short spell with Hednesford and a longer spell as manager of Coleshill, before returning again to Walsall to serve them as trainer for most of the 1980s. Stan has also made his mark in the sports equipment business.

Tall and commanding, Stan had a superb positional sense, was powerful in the air and a real threat to opposing defences when going up for set pieces.

Mick Kearns

Goalkeeper, 1973-1979 and 1982-1985

	First Team Appearances	Goals
Football League	275	0
FA Cup	24	0
FL Cup	23	0
TOTAL	322	0

Mick Kearns was not only one of Walsall's biggest and best goalkeepers of all time, but he has continued to render excellent service to the club in more recent years as community liaison officer and family co-ordinator.

Born in Banbury in 1950, Mick played for Banbury United before joining Oxford as an apprentice in 1967. He signed as a professional in 1968 and made his first-team debut in March 1970, at a time when a former Walsall player, Gerry Summers, was manager and Ron Atkinson was in the defence. In three games that season Mick kept two clean sheets, and he became first choice in the following season, playing in all 49 League and cup games after Jimmy Barron's move to Nottingham Forest. In the same season he won the first of his 18 Republic of Ireland caps.

He had the bad luck to break an ankle early in the 1972/73 season, and on his recovery he had loan spells with Plymouth and Charlton before joining Walsall for a reputed £12,000 in the summer of 1973. In the previous season Walsall had used seven different goalkeepers but, despite a 2-0 defeat in his debut at Wrexham, Mick missed only one game all campaign. He was an ever-present in 1974/75, playing in the unforgettable FA Cup wins over Manchester United and Newcastle. In fact, he went on to play in 171 successive games, possibly his finest being in a second replay in the FA Cup second round tie against Chesterfield just a few days before Christmas 1976, when Walsall won 1-0 despite being outplayed for most of the game.

In 1978/79, Ian Turner provided competition for the first-team place and Mick moved to Wolves in the summer of 1979. In the following April, he saved a penalty in a goal-less draw in his debut at The Hawthorns but, after just 10 first-team games (such was the consistency of Paul Bradshaw) Mick returned to Walsall in 1982. There he contested the first-team spot with Ron Green, at a time when his brother, Ollie, was playing up front. In the following season, Mick figured prominently in a 2-1 Milk Cup win against Arsenal at Highbury in November 1983.

Even after becoming steward at a local working men's club, Kearns returned as a non-contract player at the end of 1984/85. He then had a short spell with Worcester. 1990 saw him back at Walsall, who had just moved to the Bescot Stadium, As community officer and goalkeeping coach, he has continued to give the club first-class service. He also became a popular broadcaster with BBC Radio WM.

Standing 6ft 4in and weighing 14 stone, Mick is a big man in every sense of the word – a real gentle giant respected by people inside and outside the game.

Dean Keates

Midfielder, 1996-present

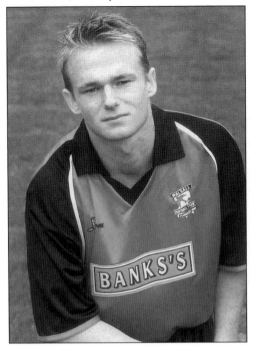

	First Team Appearances	Goals
Football League	146	8
FA Cup	11	0
FL Cup	15	1
Others	15	3
TOTAL	187	12

Over the past thirty years, Walsall have usually been able to field a busy little midfielder, and Dean Keates has proved to be a worthy successor to players such as Ray Train, Alan Birch and David Preece.

Born in Walsall in 1978, Dean graduated via the junior ranks to make his first-team debut when going on as substitute for Darren Bradley in the 1-0 defeat by Plymouth in October 1996. A few weeks later, he created a big impression when he played the whole of the game against Notts County that was won 3-1, and he was labelled by reporters as the little man with a heart bigger than his size.

He has certainly justified that tag over recent years. He established himself in 1997/98, wearing the number nine shirt but playing mainly in midfield. He got the match-winner at Millwall and also scored a spectacular AutoWindscreen goal against Brighton.

He missed only three games in the 1998/99 promotion season, adding to his reputation as a goal-snatcher with goals in successive games against Wigan and Reading but, most important of all, never allowing the opposition to settle on the ball. He added another dimension to his game in 1999/2000 when, despite standing only 5ft 6in tall, he headed goals at both Plymouth and Barnsley. It was very disappointing that his tireless running did not keep Walsall up. Undismayed, he gave of his best again in the thrilling promotion win of 2000/01. Though he was not always first choice in midfield, he was regularly brought back when more bite was needed.

There were times when he looked the complete player – not only dominating midfield, but going back in defence when the pressure was on, and at other times finding space up front and delivering perfectly placed corners and free-kicks.

As we go to press, Darren is giving his usual one hundred per cent, in an effort to keep Walsall in Division One. Still only twenty-three years of age, he has probably not yet reached his peak. Midfield players, like spin bowlers and good wine, have a habit of getting better and better with the passage of time.

David Kelly
Striker, 1983-1990

	First Team Appearances	Goals
Football League	147	63
FA Cup	15	3
FL Cup	12	4
Others	17	10
TOTAL	191	80

Although relatively short of stature for a striker, David Kelly has proved himself a superb opportunist both for Walsall and for the seven League clubs that he has served since leaving the Saddlers.

Born in Birmingham in 1965, he joined Walsall from Alvechurch midway through the 1983/84 season and made his first-team debut in what was then the new Associate Members' Cup in February 1984, going on as substitute for Alan Buckley in a 3-1 win against Northampton. Later that season, he scored in successive games against Burnley, Wigan and Plymouth. In the following season, he won a regular place up front and scored 11 goals, two of them in a thrilling 3-0 Milk Cup win at Coventry's Highfield Road.

He was something of a super-sub in the following season, with 21 of his 28 appearances coming off the bench. He still managed to score 10 goals and when Tommy Coakley succeeded Alan Buckley as manager in the summer of 1986, David became first choice for the number nine shirt. He got 26 goals in 55 games by the end of that season.

He was then the greatest single factor in the promotion of 1987/88, his tally of 30 goals including a hat-trick against Mansfield during the vital last few weeks of the League season and a hat-trick in the replayed final of the play-offs against Bristol City. If only he could have stayed at Fellows Park, Walsall would have been a fair bet to hold on to their newly-won Second Division place, but West Ham signed him for a £600,000 fee in the summer of 1988 to set up a new Walsall transfer record.

He then moved successively to Leicester in 1990 and Newcastle in 1991, banging home 28 goals in the course of their Division One championship win in 1992/93. Then it was back to the Midlands with Wolves the following summer. There he partnered Steve Bull in 1993/94, and got 14 goals. He got another 22 in 1994/95, but early in the next season he moved on to Sunderland.

There he had injury problems, and got just two goals in nearly two seasons, but he regained his scoring touch after joining Tranmere in 1997, going on to net 37 goals before moving to Sheffield United. He got 7 goals for the Blades in 2000/01, to take his career tally to 240 in just under 600 games. He has also played 26 times for the Republic of Ireland.

David's consistent goalscoring speaks for itself, but it is doubtful whether he has ever

David Kelly beats an opponent to the ball, and provides a typical example of his finishing power.

played better in his long career than in Walsall's 1987/88 promotion season when his calm finishing power with both head and feet won many a game, including the play-off replay. It is perhaps fitting that Tommy Coakley, the manager under whom his career flourished at Walsall, has in more recent times become his business partner.

Interestingly enough, David shares with two other 1980s Walsall stalwarts, goalkeeper Ron Green and midfielder Richard O'Kelly, the distinction of making the grade with the Saddlers after moving from non-League Alvechurch.

First Team	Appearances	Goals
Football League	75	25
FA Cup	7	3
FL Cup	5	2
TOTAL	87	30

George Kirby was with Walsall for only two seasons, towards the end of his much-travelled career, but he made a tremendous impact, seeming just about the most complete all-round striker that anyone could imagine.

Born in Liverpool in 1933, George graduated via the Everton junior ranks to make his first-team debut in a First Division game at Sheffield United in April 1956. He played alongside another future Walsall player, Bert Llewellyn, on several occasions the following season, and then moved to Sheffield Wednesday in March 1959 after netting 9 goals in 27 games.

He played only three games for Wednesday before moving to Plymouth just under a year later. There he got 38 goals in two and a half seasons and then joined Southampton in September 1962.

In one of his early games for the Saints, he got a hat-trick inside four minutes for them against Middlesbrough in December 1962, and he went on to get 31 goals in 73 games before moving to Coventry in March 1964. George got a hat-trick on his home debut against Oldham, but after getting 10 goals in 18 games he moved to Swansea in October 1964. Following 8 goals in 25 games there, he finally ended up at Walsall in the summer of 1965.

At the age of thirty-one, George still had some good football in him. He made his debut in a 1-0 win at Bournemouth in the opening game of 1965/66, and in his first season got 19 goals himself. He also played a major part in the development of future England man, Allan Clarke. One of George's greatest games was in January 1966, when he played a major role in Walsall's 2-0 FA Cup win at Stoke after they were reduced to ten men by a serious injury to Jimmy McMorran. He not only proved a handful for the Stoke defence but also moved back into the Walsall defence to contain the threat of Maurice Setters when the latter moved up front.

Kirby got another 11 goals the following season and then moved into American football for a spell. He ended his Football League career with Brentford in 1968/69, before teaming up again with former Walsall colleague Harry Middleton at Worcester City in 1969/70. Later he had two spells as Halifax manager and one as Watford manager – in his first spell at The Shay, he took them from the Fourth Division to the edge of the Second Division.

Later he had spells in Iceland and Saudi Arabia and, back in this country, worked as an insurance broker. Sadly, George died early in 2000. Memories of his powerful heading and surges forward with the ball at his feet still live on.

Mo Lane

Striker, 1920/21 and 1927-1929

	First Team Appearances	Goals
Football League	57	51
FA Cup	10	4
TOTAL	67	55

Moses Lane's record as a goalscorer is second to none, and one is left with two typical 'if only' thoughts. If only Walsall had hung on to him when he was first on their books, and if only he had not suffered an injury when at the height of his goalscoring power.

Born in Willenhall in 1895, he played for Willenhall Pickwick before the First World War, won the Military Medal during active service in France and Italy and then played for Willenhall Town immediately after the war. He moved to Walsall in December 1920, at a time when they were in the Birmingham League, and scored 4 goals in 10 games. However, he was not retained for the following season when Walsall moved back into the Football League and he returned to Willenhall.

Birmingham signed him in February 1922, and he went on to score 4 goals in 15 games before moving to Derby in June 1924 and playing in an FA Cup-tie at Bradford City in 1925. He then had spells with Wellington and Worcester before Walsall's manager of the time, Jimmy Torrance, signed him in the summer of 1927.

He went straight into the first team, scoring in each of his first two games against Bristol Rovers and Watford respectively in August 1927. His blistering speed helped him to 36 goals in the season, including a late-season hat-trick against Luton. He maintained this scoring touch with another hat-trick against Crystal Palace early the following season, failing to score in only two of the first ten games.

He was also the regular penalty taker at this time, but then injury struck just before the turn of the year. Although he bravely tried to come back in a game at Brentford in the following March, he was clearly struggling. He continued to play in non-League football for a few more seasons, serving Brierley Hill, Netherton and Dudley. Even at half his usual speed, he was still a handful for defences at that level.

Mo died in 1949, but fans who saw him play continued to talk of his great heart, his dual spearhead attack with George Robson and, most of all, his speed and finishing power.

Jorge Latao
Striker, 2000-present

	First Team Appearances	Goals
Football League	45	18
FA Cup	3	1
FL Cup	4	2
TOTAL	52	21

Though Jorge had played for just one season when this book went to press, his part in Walsall's promotion season was such that whatever he was destined to achieve subsequently, he had already earned a place in the history of Walsall Football Club.

Born in Oporto, Portugal, in 1974, he played for Portuguese clubs Arintes and Feirense and was studying for a Sports Science degree when Walsall made approaches to bring him to this country. He played during the first half of a pre-season game at Raith Rovers in July 2000 without his name being released to the outside world. The handful of Walsall fans present soon realized why, as the player labelled 'trialist' netted two goals, had another shot deflected home for an own goal and hit the bar with a header, all in the first half.

At that stage he was taken off, lest any other clubs nip in for his signature. In due course the player was signed for a reported £150,000, the largest fee paid out by Walsall since Alan Buckley cost £175,000 in 1979; it was then that he was identified as Jorge Latao. In another pre-season game he went on as as second-half substitute for Brett Angell against Watford at Tamworth and, although he didn't score, his skill and persistence on the ball impressed everyone. Once in possession, he was almost immoveable and his distribution and shooting also looked good.

It was no surprise when he was in the side for the opening League game of the season at Rotherham. Just two games later, he swept home a first-time right-foot shot in the Worthington Cup tie against Kidderminster. His next goal was a powerful header against Swindon followed by a looping header against Oxford and a perfectly-placed shot against Wigan.

All of which showed that he was capable of scoring in a variety of ways, though one unusual feature was that all of his first eighteen goals were scored in separate games and he did not get two in a game until near the end of the season, when he netted two accurately-placed shots against Brentford.

Although he didn't score in the play-offs, he was always a threat and his reputation as an opportunist ensured that he had maximum attention from opponents, thus creating more opportunities for colleagues. Not surprisingly, Jorge was voted Player of the Season by fans who appreciated that they had been watching one of the best all-round strikers Walsall have ever fielded.

Jackie Lewis

Goalkeeper, 1945-1953

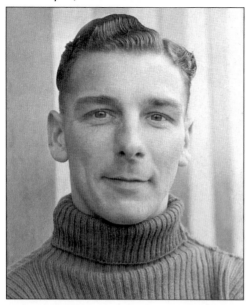

	First Team Appearances	Goals
Football League	271	0
FA Cup	15	0
TOTAL	286	0

Jackie Lewis was one of the smallest goal-keepers ever to play for Walsall, but for eight seasons he gave tremendous service and time and time again stood between Walsall and heavy defeats.

Born in Tamworth in May 1920, he played for Boldmere St Michaels during the war years and, after being tried out by Walsall manager Harry Hibbs in the public practice match of 1945/46, he was signed initially on amateur forms. He made his first-team debut in a 1-0 defeat at Northampton at the beginning of September and when Bert Williams moved to Wolves later that month, Jackie became first choice.

He missed only four games for the rest of what was the last war-time season, and helped his side reach the final of the Third Division (South) Cup, in which they lost 1-0 to Bournemouth at Stamford Bridge. Then, when normal League football was resumed in 1946, Jackie missed only four games in five seasons. Amongst many outstanding displays, two of the most memorable were in the city of Nottingham early in 1949/50. At Forest's City Ground, he limited the home side to a 1-0 win and at County's Meadow Lane in front of a 42,000 gate he defied all that Tommy Lawton and others threw at him until the very last minute, when Lawton netted a very doubtful

penalty to level the scores at 1-1.

No greater tribute can be given to Jackie Lewis than that his brilliance in the late 1940s and early '50s was such that Bert Williams, who had moved on to win League Championship and FA Cup honours with Wolves and to play 24 times for England, was not really missed. Jackie finally came under challenge from Gordon Chilvers in the 1952/53 season and moved on to Hereford in the following summer. There he remained for two seasons, before moving to Bromsgrove to ease the travelling.

He played several times for Bromsgrove in Birmingham League games against Walsall, and in March 1958 (aged nearly thirty-eight) he played a major role in a 3-1 win against a Walsall reserve side that included an up-and-coming Stan Jones in defence and Colin Taylor up front. Then, when Kidderminster had a goalkeeping problem, Jackie came out of retirement to play for them for half of 1964/65, aged forty-four but still with a safe pair of hands.

For many years Jackie kept the White Hart in Atherstone and helped with boys' teams who played near his hostelry. Sadly, he died in 1988, but many still talk of his uncanny anticipation, his agility and calmness under pressure and his speed from his goal. Although standing only 5ft 8in high, he proved undisputably that if a player is good enough then he is big enough.

Kyle Lightbourne
Striker, 1993-1997

	First Team Appearances	Goals
Football League	165	65
FA Cup	18	11
FL Cup	8	1
Others	7	6
TOTAL	198	83

When they heard Walsall had signed Kyle Lightbourne, initially on trial, after his release from Scarborough, none of the club's fans became over-excited, but within a few weeks of his arrival they were chanting his name as he revealed once again that there are bargains to be found in football if scouts and managers have the skill to find them.

Born in Bermuda in 1968, Kyle was already twenty-four when he tried his luck in this country, moving from PHC (Bermuda) in the autumn of 1992. Tall, mobile and good with his head, he played in 19 games that season and scored 3 goals, one of them in a 4-1 win over Walsall in March. He was not retained, however, at the end of the season, as Boro had something of a clear-out following the resignation of chairman Geoffrey Richmond.

Early the following season, he moved to Walsall, who remembered that goal against them. He made his debut in a goal-less draw at Darlington, going on as substitute for Mike Cecere and then in his first full game he netted in a 3-3 draw against Hereford. His mobility and skill on the ball were two of the bright spots in an otherwise undistinguished season, in which he ended up top scorer with 9 goals, as Walsall ended up in tenth spot in Division Three.

He was one of the players whom Chris Nicholl inherited when taking over as manager, and Kyle welcomed his new boss with a hat-trick in a 5-1 win over Fulham. His season's tally was 27 as he helped his side to promotion and was selected for the Division Three team at the PFA awards ceremony. He scored almost as freely in Division Two in 1995/96, becoming the first Walsall player to score four goals in a game since Alan Buckley twenty years earlier when he did so against Wycome in the Auto Windscreen. His season's tally was 24, despite being troubled with a groin injury.

1996/97 saw him finishing as the club's leading scorer for the third successive season and he gave up the chance of adding to his 24 Bermuda caps in order to play for Walsall in the (vain) late bid for a play-off place.

He moved to Coventry for a reported £500,000 in July 1997, but after just 10 games and a spell on loan to Fulham he moved to Stoke in the following February. He had problems with illness and injury in his first few months at Stoke. He came good, however, in 1999/2000, as he formed an effective dual spearhead with Peter Thorne, totalled 10 goals and helped his side to the AutoWindscreen Trophy. He scored just 3 goals in 2000/01 and when he was out of the team, rumours suggested that he might be on his way back to Walsall. This didn't happen, but Walsall fans do hold in high regard a player of genuine pace, calm finishing power and with great headwork, who stands in seventh place in the all-time list of Walsall scorers.

Doug Lishman

Striker, 1946-1948

	First Team Appearances	Goals
Football League	59	25
FA Cup	6	4
TOTAL	64	29

Doug Lishman was with Walsall for just two seasons, but ranks amongst the very greatest strikers to have worn the club colours.

Born in Birmingham in 1923, he played in local junior football before the war and then gave distinguished service with the Royal Marine Commandos, taking part in the Walcheren landing in Holland. When hostilities ceased he played for Paget Rangers and was spotted by then Walsall manager Harry Hibbs. He was signed in time for the start of the first season of normal League football after the war.

He scored in the first thirty seconds of a public practice match and a week later got two of the goals in a reserve game against the West Brom third team. Fans were soon clamouring for him to be in the first team, but manager Harry Hibbs did not rush things and Doug was finally selected for an FA Cup replay at Ipswich in December 1946. He responded by getting the match-winner in the second half, with a perfect header from a Jackie Maund cross.

Doug also scored in his first League game, against Notts County on the following Saturday, and later that season got two goals in the remarkable 8-0 win at Northampton on Easter Tuesday. His excellent form continued into the following season, when he got 20 goals, including seven in the last six games. It was inevitable that Doug would be the target of First Division clubs, and Arsenal signed him for a reported £10,500 in May 1948. He was in and out of the team in his first two seasons, but then in 1950/51 he really came good, getting 16 goals, before breaking a leg in a Christmas Day game.

He was back as good as ever before the end of the season, and in eight years with Arsenal scored 135 goals in 243 games, won a First Division Championship medal, an FA Cup runners-up medal and played for the England 'B' team. He moved to Nottingham Forest in March 1956, and in just over a season with them scored 22 goals in 38 games, ending on a high note with a hat-trick (the ninth of his career) in his last away game at Sheffield United.

Doug then went into the family furniture business in the Potteries and worked there for the rest of his days.

Doug died in 1994, and there is no finer tribute to this great striker than when Allan Clarke began showing the sort of form that was to win him 19 England caps, and fans began to label him 'our best striker since Doug Lishman'.

Doug Lishman is pictured here (extreme right, front row) at the beginning of the 1947/48 season, when Walsall were strong promotion candidates for much of the campaign. Doug was a key figure in a prolific forward line that chalked up five wins in a row in October and November. Things were never quite the same after Dave Massart's move to Bury in March, and when Doug moved to Arsenal in the following close season, promotion hopes vanished. Walsall had to wait another thirteen years before getting into the Second Division.

Rod McDonald

Striker, 1990-1994

	First Team Appearances	Goals
Football League	149	41
FA Cup	8	2
FL Cup	9	2
Others	12	1
TOTAL	178	46

Rod McDonald was an exciting striker on his day, and he gave Walsall fans something to cheer about at a time when in general things were not going particularly well for the team as a whole.

Born in London in 1967, Rod McDonald first attracted attention while playing for Colne Dynamos, the Northern club who won the HFS Loans League in 1989/90 and then folded. This left Rod without a club of any kind. Although he had not had any Football League experience until then and was already twenty-three, Kenny Hibbitt, who was seeking to build a new Walsall after relegation in successive seasons, gave him his big chance. Walsall had just moved into the new Bescot Stadium, but at the time when Rod made his debut they had failed to win any of their first seven League games.

Rod went on as substitute for Peter Bodak after the latter had scored in a 3-0 win over Scunthorpe. Then, in his first full game, McDonald found the net in a 3-1 win at Maidstone. He did seem to be something of a lucky omen and a few weeks later he scored the match-winner in an FA Cup tie at Aylesbury.

He continued to progress, and in 1991/92 was far and away the leading Walsall scorer with 17 goals, including a fine Boxing Day hat-trick against Blackpool. Playing on the left flank of the attack, he missed only three games in 1992/93 and got another 13 goals in a season in which he gave good support to Wayne Clarke and Mike Cecere as Walsall reached the Division Three play-offs.

He was less prolific in 1993/94, as he scored just 8 goals, playing up front alongside Kyle Lightbourne for the most part. He moved to Partick Thistle for a reported £30,000 fee in September 1994, scored 12 goals for them in just under two seasons and then had a short spell with Southport in the first three months of the 1996/97 season. He totalled 12 goals before being released in the summer of 1998. More recently, he had a short spell with Northwich in the Conference.

Rod McDonald has proved himself something of a nomad, and Walsall fans probably saw him at his best. Like many other strikers, he was a delight when things were going well but could show a fiery side when he felt he was being unfairly treated.

	First Team Appearances	Goals
Football League	104	10
FA Cup	9	0
FL Cup	7	0
TOTAL	120	10

McMorran was one of the most skilful ball players that Walsall have ever fielded and it was unfortunate that this same skill made him the target of some ruthless opponents, with the result that he suffered more than his share of injuries and at times exploded into retaliation.

Born in Ayr in 1942, Jimmy was capped by Scotland at schoolboy level and came south to Aston Villa aged just sixteen, signing professionally in 1959.

He was still only seventeen when he made his Aston Villa debut against Cardiff, and then a week later helped them to a 3-1 win over Manchester United. He totalled 14 games for Villa (scoring a goal against Blackpool in February 1962) before moving to Third Lanark in 1963 and coming south again to Walsall early in November 1964, soon after Bill Harrison had taken over as chairman.

He made his debut in a 2-1 defeat at Oldham in November 1964, and a week later played in one of the games of the season – a 4-3 win over Brentford. He missed only one match for the rest of the campaign, got a match-winner at Bristol Rovers, and then in the following season displayed his silky skills week after week until he was seriously injured by a heavy tackle in an FA Cup tie at Stoke, which Walsall went on to win with ten men.

Jimmy was back in top form again early in 1967/68, when Walsall seemed to be romping to promotion, and he also slipped home the occasional penalty around this time. Sadly, the promotion bid faded during chairman Bill Harrison's terminal illness, and Jimmy moved to Swansea Town (as they were then) in the summer of 1968. He returned a few months later in exchange for Alfie Biggs and played a splendid game in an FA Cup tie against Spurs, in which Jimmy Greaves got the winner against the run of play.

Jimmy moved on again, this time to Notts County, in 1969. He ended his League career with Halifax and then did the rounds of the Midland non-League sides, his clubs including Worcester, Redditch and Hednesford. More recently he has had a spell as manager of Darlaston, whom he left in 2000.

Anyone who didn't see Jimmy McMorran's skill on the ball in his heyday missed a real treat.

Albert McPherson

Central defender, 1954-1964

	First Team Appearances	Goals
Football League	351	8
FA Cup	12	0
FL Cup	4	0
TOTAL	367	8

Major Buckley made many signings in the mid-1950s as he desperately tried to find a winning formula for a side that had been forced to apply for re-election four seasons in succession. None of them were better than Albert McPherson, who turned out to be one of the best central defenders the club have ever had.

Born in Salford in 1927, he was on Bury's books in the late 1940s but did not break through into the first team. He then had a couple of seasons with one-time Football League club Stalybridge Celtic in the Cheshire League, and it was their manager, Harry Chapman, who told him to try again in the Football League.

Albert, at the age of twenty-seven, desperately needed another chance. Walsall needed a top class defender – it was fortunate indeed that the two linked up. Albert signed in the summer of 1954. He made his first-team debut in a 2-0 home defeat by Brighton at the beginning of the following September. He won a regular place in the latter part of that season and missed only a handful of games for the next few seasons. He was very much the man for the

occasion, and in a Monday evening game against Northampton in April 1956, when Walsall needed all the points they could get in order to avoid a fifth successive re-election application, Albert calmly slotted home two penalties to win the game. Just four years later, he found himself featuring prominently in Walsall's Fourth Division championship side. When Harry Haddington suffered a broken leg early the following season, Albert took over as captain and led the side to promotion again.

He continued to hold his own in Walsall's first season back in the Second Division in 1961/62, playing in every League game for the first time in his career. Although he lost his place to Tony Eden for a brief spell in the 1962/63 relegation season, and to Ron Howells in the 1963/64 season back in the Third Division, Albert came back each time to end the season in top form. He was just two months short of thirty-seven when he retired from League football in the summer of 1967.

After a short spell with Stourbridge, he was on the West Brom training staff from 1964 to 1984, coaching at different times the first team, the reserves and the youth team. A gentleman both on and off the field, Albert McPherson was a credit to the game throughout his long career.

Albert McPherson leads Walsall out from the Fellows Park dressing room, followed by Ken Hill. As team captain, McPherson was an inspiration on the field, being a model of consistency himself and having the ability to get the best out of his colleagues. Off the field, he was a splendid ambassador for the club.

Peter McSevich

Goalkeeper, 1933-1936

	First Team Appearances	Goals
Football League	102	0
FA Cup	11	0
FL Cup	8	0
TOTAL	121	0

Peter McSevich was not only one of the finest goalkeepers to play for Walsall over the years, but served the club behind the scenes for many years after his retirement.

Born in Stevenston, Ayrshire, in 1908, he won two Scottish junior international caps during his early days with Celtic in the mid-1920s, moved on to Aberdeen in 1925 and, after 36 games for them, travelled all the way to the South Coast to link up with Bournemouth in 1928. One of his first games for the Cherries was a 2-1 defeat by Walsall. He missed just two games in 1929/30 and played in every game in 1930/31, one of them a real thriller against Walsall, which ended 3-3.

Peter was the sort of goalkeeper who had adventures. In a game at Brighton in October 1931, he was injured and went into the forward line (as injured goalkeepers sometimes did in those pre-substitute days) and actually scored a goal. What is more, he was fit to play again a week later, although he ended up on the wrong side of a 6-1 defeat at Coventry.

Coventry's manager, the redoubtable Harry Storer, must have been impressed with Peter nevertheless, as he signed him the following summer after a total of 142 games for the Cherries. He did well enough in the course of 38 games for the Bantams (as they were then), several of them in the same line-up as Bill Sheppard and Ben Woolhouse, who were also destined to land up at Walsall. In the last few games of 1932/33, however, he lost his place to rising star Bill Morgan, and moved on to Walsall in the following summer.

He replaced Joe Cunningham, one of the heroes of the FA Cup win over Arsenal, just a few games into the season, making his debut in a 3-2 defeat at Carlisle. Both Joe and Peter had been juniors at Aberdeen in the 1920s. From the time he came into the side, Peter missed only four games in nearly two and a half years.

Although he made the occasional slip, he was at his best when the going was tough. He starred in the FA Cup win over Watford in December 1934, when Walsall went through 1-0 at Fellows Park after a goal-less draw at Vicarage Road. He also played a major part in the run to the Third Division (North) Cup final when Walsall eventually lost 2-0 to Stockport at Maine Road.

Injury in a game at Southport in February 1936, when he fractured a collarbone in a collision with a home forward, ended his excellent run. After a short spell with Wellington, he retired from the active game. Following the war, he served Walsall for many years as youth-team coach and dressing-room attendant, living within a few yards of Fellows Park until his death in 1982. He remained popular with fans and there was an occasion in the 1970s when he was standing near the dressing rooms as a Walsall 'keeper was having a poor game. One raucous spectator called out: 'Get back between them posts, Peter'.

Tony Macken

Defender, 1977-1982

	First Team Appearances	Goals
Football League	190	1
FA Cup	15	1
FL Cup	9	0
TOTAL	214	2

Tony Macken was one of a handful of Republic of Ireland internationals to have played for Walsall over the years, proving himself as a neat, consistent, right-flank defender during his five years with the club.

Born in Dublin in 1950, he played for his hometown club before joining Derby in 1974, when Dave Mackay was manager. While at the Baseball Ground, he was first tried as a defender and also had two loan spells with Portsmouth, playing in a total of 10 games for Pompey. He was also capped for the Republic of Ireland against Spain in 1977. He had loan spells with Washington Diplomats and Dallas Tornados in the summers of 1976 and 1977, and then joined Walsall in October 1977, linking up again with his former Derby manager, Dave Mackay.

Tony's debut was on the right flank of the defence in a game at Chesterfield that Walsall won 1-0. He played regularly from that point on, as Walsall experienced mixed fortunes. He took part in the FA Cup victory over Leicester in January 1978, followed by a brave display in a 4-1 defeat by Arsenal at Highbury. Then, in the unhappy relegation season of 1978/79, he played occasionally in midfield and on the left flank of defence, but always returned to his accustomed right-flank slot.

He missed only four games in the 1979/80 promotion season, and it was in the course of that campaign that he scored his one and only League goal for the club – and what an important one it was. It set Walsall on the way to victory at promotion-rivals Portsmouth in front of a 21,785 gate at Fratton Park. Tony also played in the dramatic 2-1 win at Bramall Lane right at the end of the 1980/81 season, to keep Walsall up and send Sheffield United down. In fact, his last game in Walsall's colours was right at the end of the 1981/82 season, when there was a march to the ground by fans protesting at the plans to move the club to Birmingham.

Tony then went back to Waterford, and later played for Home Farm when approaching the age of forty. A very neat, determined little player, Tony is remembered for his consistency at what was something of a roller-coaster spell in the history of Walsall Football Club.

Norman Male

Left-flank defender, 1938-1949

	First Team Appearances	Goals
Football League	70	2
FA Cup	10	0
Others	1	0
TOTAL	81	2

Norman Male is remembered as a fine club servant, not only for his efforts as a player, which were ended prematurely by injury, but also for his later dedicated service as reserve-team trainer.

Born in West Bromwich in 1917, he played for Bush Rangers before being snapped up by West Brom. After a spell as a junior, he signed as a professional in 1934. He won junior international honours for England in 1935 and made his first-team debut on the right flank of the defence in the First Division game at Grimsby in September 1937, scoring one of the goals in a 3-1 win.

He played just three first-team games, before moving to Walsall in 1938 and making his debut in a 3-1 defeat at Brighton on the opening day of the 1938/39 season. He played in the FA Cup run that season, when Walsall reached the fifth round for the first time. He then featured during the war years, figuring regularly as defensive partner to Jack Shelton. There was a feeling of confidence for fans as the two distinctive figures lined up, Jack with the sleeked-down hair and Norman with the balding pate.

All in all Norman played in 184 wartime games, but when normal football was resumed in 1946/47, the young Irvine Methley and Bill Skidmore had arrived from Wolves and Norman lost his place for a time.

Back he came, however, to play regularly in 1947/48, looking as good as ever with his accurate clearances and fine positional play. He was playing regularly again in the early part of 1948/49, when he suffered a serious knee injury in a quite remarkable game against Millwall. The visitors lost 'keeper Malcolm Finlayson with a first-half injury and Walsall lost Norman with injury as well. Both returned, however, Malcolm playing bravely in the visitors' goal and Norman moving into the Walsall front line and scoring two goals. The game ended 6-5, but far more serious was the fact that Norman was never fit for League football again.

He did serve the club for another twenty-two years, however, most of them as reserve-team trainer. A salt-of-the-earth character, Norman was a great club servant who had an unusual distinction. He scored his only three League goals in his first and last games, one on his debut and two in his final match.

	First Team Appearances	Goals
Football League	392	23
FA Cup	36	3
FL Cup	25	1
Others	25	3
TOTAL	478	30

Chris Marsh was one of the breed of players who had become increasingly rare as the game moved into the twenty-first century – the ones who give more than ten years of service to the same club.

Born in Sedgley in 1970, Chris joined Walsall on a YTS scheme and made his first-team debut as a seventeen year old, going on as substitute for Nicky Cross in January 1988. He banged the ball into the net with his first kick, but the referee disallowed the effort because someone else was offside. Chris signed professionally in the following summer, and for a time played mainly as substitute as Walsall tried to get their act together again in the Fourth Division at the new Bescot Stadium, after relegation in successive seasons.

Chris got his first goal to win the game against Doncaster in February 1991, and then in 1991/92 he played at various times in attack, midfield and defence. He was in the team that reached the Division Three play-offs in 1992/93, and then two years later enjoyed probably his best-ever season, missing only four games in midfield and scoring nine of the goals that took Walsall to promotion. He also netted a fine goal against Leeds in the FA Cup, which deserved a better fate than to be wiped out by a late equalizer.

He was club captain in the first season in Division Two in 1995/96, and would probably have been an ever-present but for an unlucky sending-off in a game at Notts County. 1996/97 saw him enjoying a benefit season and playing bravely in goal at Chesterfield after Jimmy Walker had been sent off. He had another spell in goal at Northampton late in December 1997, after Jimmy Walker had been carried off. By this time he was playing regularly in defence, but near the end of another excellent season in 1998/99, he moved forward to get the second goal against Oldham in the game that clinched promotion.

In Division One, he again played bravely in 1999/2000, giving his all despite a nagging Achilles injury. He also spent most of the game in goal against Barnsley after Jimmy Walker had been sent off. A close-season operation seemed to have cleared up his injury worries and he appeared to be easing his way back into the side around the turn of the year. Fans were disappointed, therefore, when he was transferred to Wycombe early in 2001, and feelings were mixed when the news came through that he had been Man of the Match in one of his first appearances for his new club.

Chris Marsh takes the ball between two opponents in a typical surge forward.

Chris Marsh personified all that was best in Walsall football in modern times and fans will never forget his enthusiastic surges forward out of defence or his famous step-over to wrong-foot an opponent. Only five players have made more appearances for Walsall over the years.

At the time of writing, Chris had moved to Northampton Town, linking up again with former Walsall team-mate, Kevin Wilson. When Kevin was sacked, Chris's future looked a little uncertain, though one has the feeling that there is still some good football in him.

	First Team Appearances	Goals
Football League	27	3
FA Cup	2	0
TOTAL	29	23

Dave Massart played for Walsall for only just over half a season, but was still being talked of over fifty years later because of the scoring burst with which he arrived on the Fellows Park scene.

Born in Birmingham in 1919, he linked up with his home-city club before the war, signing professionally in 1939 and scoring 18 goals in 20 wartime games. He played in just three games in the Second Division in the first post-war season of 1946/47, and in the following summer was signed by Harry Hibbs, the former Birmingham goalkeeper who was then manager of Walsall.

No player has made a more dramatic start in Walsall's colours, as in his first two games Dave got hat-tricks against Exeter and Leyton Orient respectively. He then got another in the next home game against Southend, thus chalking up 9 goals in his first 3 games at Fellows Park.

He continued to score steadily, and on 1 November 1947, he got all four goals in a 4-0 win at Brighton that left home fans demonstrating against their side's inability to stop him. Things slowed down a little after that, as Dave missed a few games through injury. To the disappointment of fans, he was transferred to Bury just before transfer deadline day.

This meant that he was moving up a division, but Dave nevertheless scored on his debut in a 3-3 draw at West Brom and went on to get 47 goals in 89 games for the Shakers. He moved to Chesterfield in February 1951, scored 5 goals in 11 games and was then transferred to Southern League club Weymouth. There he scored freely for a couple of seasons, before standing as a Tory candidate in local elections.

He later kept a sub-post office and after that became an hotelier. Sadly, Dave died in 1993. Older fans can still picture his powerful physique, the way he turned an opponent and the way he made a bee-line for goal and usually ended with a powerful shot. He was the epitome of the old-fashioned centre forward.

Pedro Matias

Midfielder, 1999-present

	First Team Appearances	Goals
Football League	73	16
FA Cup	4	1
FL Cup	3	0
Others	1	0
TOTAL	81	17

Pedro has the distinction of being a former Real Madrid player but (more importantly for Walsall fans) he is also the man who played a major role in their 2000/01 promotion win.

Born in Madrid in 1973, he won Spanish under-21 international honours before coming to this country to try his luck with Macclesfield in 1998, having previously played for Spanish clubs Logrones, Almeria and Real Madrid. He did not speak any English at the time, but created an immediate impression with some great runs from midfield. He laid on a number of goals before finally getting on the score-sheet himself with a goal against Stoke.

However, he was released by Macclesfield after 22 games and was taken on a three-month trial by Tranmere in the summer of 1999. He made only 4 appearances for them, before Walsall picked him up on a free transfer in the following October. He made an impressive debut in a Friday evening win over Birmingham and earned a regular place. Walsall fans were thrilled to see the way he went past opponents, and his made-to-measure crosses were also a great asset. It was an added bonus that he occasionally came up with a spectacular goal, such as the perfect chip shot against Fulham that was captured for Sky TV viewers.

After being one of Walsall's most successful players in Division One, people wondered just how he would fit into Division Two in 2000/01. Happily, he did well, and it was an indication of his strong all-round game that his first three goals of the season were scored with his supposedly weaker right foot.

Pedro had two particularly memorable games as Walsall closed in on promotion. In the game against Wycombe in late March, he got a hat-trick with a well-placed shot, a spectacular volley and a diving header. Then in the play-off semi-final against Stoke, he scored with a perfect angled shot and then got a second goal by harrying a defender into kicking the ball against him and it rebounding into the net.

A total of 11 goals in the season underline just how far he has developed into a goal-scoring midfielder. Walsall fans are hoping that in the 2000/01 season there will be many more where those came from.

George Meek

Winger, 1954/55 and 1961-1965

	First Team Appearances	Goals
Football League	172	28
FA Cup	10	1
FL Cup	5	0
TOTAL	187	29

George Meek was a diminutive winger with skill galore and abundant energy, who had two successful spells with Walsall, one in the mid-1950s and one in the early 1960s.

Born in Glasgow in 1934, he was playing for Hamilton Academicals when Major Frank Buckley signed him for Leeds in the summer of 1952. Although only eighteen years old, he played 28 games, alternating between the right and left wings. He scored 5 goals that season and then, while doing his National Service in the Royal Armoured Corps, he was taken on loan by his former Leeds boss Major Buckley, who by that time was in charge at Walsall.

He scored on his Walsall debut in a 2-0 win over QPR in January 1954, and he was rarely out of the team until he was recalled to Leeds in February 1955. He played in more than half the games in the 1955/56 promotion season and was virtually an ever-present in the next two seasons as they established themselves in the First Division. He had scored 19 goals in 199 games for Leeds by the time he moved to Leicester in the summer of 1960. With two more future Walsall players, Howard Riley and Gordon Wills, competing for the wing spots, George played just 13 games the following season and he welcomed the chance to return to Walsall in the summer of 1961.

Walsall had just won promotion to the Second Division. George got into the side for the third game of the season (a 3-1 win at Derby) and made the number seven shirt his own, scoring 9 goals to leave him third in the season's scoring list, behind the prolific Tony Richards and Colin Taylor.

He missed only two games in the following season, as Walsall so unluckily slipped to relegation, George running his heart out in a vain bid to turn the tide in that fatal last game against Charlton. He played regularly until November 1964, and then lost his place when new chairman Bill Harrison and new manager Ray Shaw revamped the club.

George then had a short spell with Dudley and a long spell with Rushall Olympic, whom he served until he reached his fifties. One of his jobs outside football was as a postman, and in the 1980s he was to be seen delivering letters up and down the Bloxwich Road, moving almost as well as when he ran down the Walsall right and left wings.

George Meek was a little man with a big heart, twinkling toes and a powerful finish.

Irvine Methley

Defender, 1945-1951

	First Team Appearances	Goals
Football League	113	0
FA Cup	8	0
TOTAL	121	0

Irvine Methley was one of many skilful young players who moved from Wolves to Walsall just after the Second World War. He was an outstanding defender, whose career was unfortunately curtailed by injury.

Born in Barnsley in 1925, he played for Wath Wanderers and then moved south to play for Wolves in a wartime game against Leicester in December 1942, playing at that time in midfield as he did in all his three games for Wolves. When he joined Walsall in 1945, however, he went straight to the right flank of the defence, making his debut in a 1-0 defeat at Port Vale in January 1946 and partnering first Norman Male and then Jack Shelton. He held his place for the rest of that season, and played in the Third Division (South) Cup final, in which Walsall went down to Bournemouth at Stamford Bridge.

When normal divisional football was resumed in August 1946, Methley played in every game in that first post-war season and was heading in the same direction in 1947/48 when he twisted a knee in a game against Notts County. He hobbled on the wing (as injured players often did in those pre-substitute days)

and almost scored, but the injury was to keep him out of the team until the following October and, in all honesty, he was never quite the same player again.

At different times he played on both flanks of the defence and on the right-hand side of midfield, and his powerful clearances were always a feature of his game. He stayed with Walsall until 1951, and then played from 1951 to 1953 for Northwich Victoria in the Cheshire League. However, with his knee still causing him trouble, he retired from the game at the age of twenty-seven.

For many years he kept a fish and chip business in Leamore, and chatted to customers about how privileged he was to have played in that 1945/46 Walsall team, with the outstanding half-back line of Crutchley, Foulkes and Newman and ace schemer Les Talbot in the front line. Customers would then share their own memories of the Methley-Skidmore full-back partnership that repelled many an attack in the late 1940s. Think back to the stout-hearted defenders that have played for Walsall and one thinks immediately of Irvine Methley.

Colin Methven
Defender, 1990-1993

	First Team Appearances	Goals
Football League	97	3
FA Cup	5	0
FL Cup	6	0
Others	9	0
TOTAL	117	3

Colin Methven was well into his thirty-eighth year when he played his last game for Walsall in April 1993, and so was the oldest player to appear for them since the Second World War. He is remembered, however, as a commanding defender whose balding pate and powerful heading brought back memories for older fans of Lew Morgan in pre-war days.

Born in India in 1955, Colin made his entry into the professional soccer scene with East Fife, playing for them in a game against Stranraer at the end of the 1974/75 season. He was an ever-present for them until moving to Wigan for £30,000 in September 1979. He made his debut for them against Doncaster in a Fourth Division game a month later, and remained for the next two seasons.

Soon he was captaining the side and he was Player of the Year in both 1979/80 and 1984/85. He was chosen by his fellow professionals for the Fourth Division select team in 1981/82. In total, Methven played 340 times for the Latics and scored 28 goals, before moving to Blackpool in 1986. He had four excellent seasons at Bloomfield Road, missing only 10 League games during that time and showing outstanding leadership qualities, as well as power in defence and when going forward.

Blackpool fans were not pleased when new manager Graham Carr released him in the summer of 1990, saying that he was neither fast enough nor good enough for Fourth Division football. How those words rebounded when Carr was sacked after just four months and Methven signed for Walsall in November 1990 after a two-month spell on loan to Carlisle. Kenny Hibbitt was striving to improve the Walsall defence that had kept only two clean sheets in fourteen games after moving in at Bescot.

Colin made an immediate impact, partnering Dean Smith in a 1-0 win over Burnley in his debut game. In only his third game, he snatched the vital second goal in a 2-2 draw at Chesterfield and he did not miss a single game for the rest of the season. He enjoyed a particular triumph in the last game, when Walsall beat Blackpool 2-0 in front of a 8,000 Bescot gate to rob the Seasiders of automatic promotion.

He missed only two games in 1991/92 and, though he did not command quite such a regular place in 1992/93, he showed what a good club-man he was by filling in on the left flank of the defence on a number of occasions when Steph O'Hara was partnering Dean Smith in the centre.

He moved out in 1993, and later became a hotelier. Colin's zeal for the game was a splendid example to all, and during his time at Walsall he proved that if a player is still good enough, he is never too old.

Lew Morgan

Central defender, 1934-1939

	First Team Appearances	Goals
Football League	192	1
FA Cup	21	0
Others	11	0
TOTAL	224	1

Lew Morgan was a dominant defender whose balding forehead cleared many a long ball into the Walsall goalmouth in the years immediately before the Second World War.

Born in Aberdare in 1909, Lew Morgan played in Welsh junior football before linking up with Charlton Athletic in 1930 and making his first-team debut in a game against Millwall in September of that year.

There was keen competition for defensive spots at The Valley in those days, but Lew played 44 times in two seasons before moving to Bradford City in July 1932.

He played just once for them and then, after a season in which he played 18 times for Aldershot, he moved to Walsall in the summer of 1934. He played out of position in midfield on his debut against Hartlepool on the opening day of the following season, but soon he was making the number five shirt his own. However, in emergency he did occasionally move to the left flank of the defence, with George Leslie coming back into the centre.

Lew succeeded Billy Bradford as captain in 1935, and it was in that season that Walsall attracted a 19,000 gate for an FA Cup tie against Newcastle that they lost 2-0. It is perhaps for the FA Cup ties that he is best remembered. In the previous season, Walsall had beaten Watford after a replay and Lew's wife's vociferous support from just behind the Watford directors had occasioned comment. Also memorable were the Charlie Bulger match-winner on Yeovil's sloping pitch in December 1936, the run to the fifth round for the first time in 1939 and the defeat at Huddersfield (who had won the trophy the previous season).

Lew continued to play regularly while he was a police reserve during the Second World War, totalling 109 games during that period. After the war, Lew was reserve-team trainer for two seasons, playing one game against Darlaston in 1947, which was his only reserve-team game during the whole of his time with Walsall. Later he became managing director of Packing Supplies Ltd in Chuckery, and was a keen member of Great Barr Golf Club.

Lew died in 1979, but he is still remembered as the defender who in his prime played against some of the top strikers of the day – including Hughie Gallacher, Dixie Dean and Pongo Waring – and usually gave as good as he got.

Fred Morris

Winger/midfielder, 1950-1957

	First Team Appearances	Goals
Football League	213	44
FA Cup	17	5
TOTAL	230	49

Fred Morris was one player who brightened the scene at Fellows Park during a period in which Walsall had to apply for re-election in no fewer than four successive seasons. Fast and fearless, there were times when it seemed he would inevitably collide with the wall at the famous laundry end as he raced down the slope.

Born in Oswestry in 1929, he played for his hometown club before signing for Walsall in 1950. He made his debut in the opening game of the following season, a 2-1 defeat at Reading, but National Service restricted his appearances in the next two seasons. He really came into his own in 1952/53, when he missed only eight games. In the following three seasons he was an ever-present despite lots of changes all around him, as in successive seasons Walsall used thirty-three, thirty and twenty-seven different players.

He played mainly on the right wing, but was always ready to have a go down the opposite flank or in the centre of the attack. Just after scoring a hat-trick at Brighton from the right-wing spot, he was given an extended run by Major Buckley in midfield, where his non-stop running often kept Walsall in with a chance when otherwise they might have been overrun.

He was enjoying one of his best seasons in 1956/57, with 7 goals in 18 games, including two each at Brentford and Bournemouth in the space of five days, when he was transferred to Mansfield for a reported £1,500. He did well enough at Field Mill (17 goals in 56 games) for Liverpool manager Phil Taylor to sign him for £7,000 in the summer of 1958.

He had two good seasons there, playing in the same line-up as men like Ronnie Moran, Jimmy Melia and veteran Billy Liddell (who had played against Walsall in an FA Cup tie in 1947). He scored 14 goals in 47 games, before having short spells with Gillingham, Chester, Altrincham and Oswestry, where he was player-manager of the club where he had started his career.

Later in life he kept a garage in Oswestry, but was often to be seen at games in the West Midlands, particularly when Liverpool were the visitors. Sadly, Fred died in his seventieth year in 1999. No one had displayed more energy than him in his playing days, and he was one of the main reasons why Walsall's gates regularly topped the 10,000 mark when the team's results were very disappointing.

Kenny Mower
Defender, 1978-1991

	First Team Appearances	Goals
Football League	415	8
FA Cup	31	2
FL Cup	38	0
Others	10	0
TOTAL	494	10

Kenny Mower was a one-club man who was a worthy successor to that great band of loyal, one-club men of the 1960s (Frank Gregg, Stan Bennett, Nick Atthey and Colin Harrison). In fact, Kenny was born in 1960, just as the aforementioned players were starting their professional careers.

Kenny first attracted attention while a pupil of the T.P. Riley School. After a spell as an amateur, he signed professionally in November 1978 and made his first-team debut in the 4-1 defeat at Rotherham right at the end of the 1978/79 season, as Walsall slipped into the Fourth Division after picking up only four points from their previous twelve games.

Happily, 1979/80 was another story, as Kenny missed only two games as Walsall romped to promotion, clinching it with a 2-0 win over Tranmere on Easter Monday when Kenny scored the opening goal. In the Third Division, Kenny continued to play steadily in defence and he became a great crosser of the ball after moving up on the overlap. He played in all 9 games of that unforgettable run to the Milk Cup semi-final in 1983/84, and season after season he missed only the occasional game. Even when he had to miss the replay of the fifth round FA Cup tie against Watford in 1987, he joined the BBC Radio WM commentary team for the 4-4 draw at Vicarage Road, and then played in the second replay at Fellows Park.

He had experienced promotion and then two relegations, all in the space of three seasons, by the time he was released in 1991. He played in the first-ever game at Bescot against Torquay in August 1990, and his last game as a Walsall player was at Scunthorpe in March 1991.

Still aged only thirty, Kenny had a spell with Stafford Rangers and then joined Blakenall, playing within a mile of where he had gone to school and within two miles of where he had lived most of his life. Kenny was one of Walsall's most consistent defenders of modern times, and throughout the 1980s, fans were thrilled by his exciting dashes down the left flank.

Albert Mullard

Striker/midfielder, 1945-1949

	First Team Appearances	Goals
Football League	61	13
FA Cup	6	1
TOTAL	67	14

Albert Mullard was one of the most under-rated players to have played for Walsall over the years. Discerning fans said 'I told you so' when his career flourished for many years after leaving Fellows Park.

Born in Walsall in 1920, he played for Hinckley United as a teenager and linked up with Walsall as a junior before the war. During the hostilities he served in the Royal Marines and was a prisoner of war in Germany for four years. Happily, he came back after the war, determined to make a success of life on and off the field after wondering for so long whether he would survive.

His initial first-team game was at Watford in October 1945, in that intermediate season before League football was resumed. He played a major part in that famous run to the final of the Third Division (South) Cup, getting a total of five goals in the two legs of the quarter-final against Northampton, but ending up on the losing side in the final.

He was in the team for the first League match after the war (a 3-1 defeat at Southend), and in the course of that season he got 10 goals in 27 games, playing at various times as a striker, a winger and a midfielder. He got a hat-trick in the famous 8-0 Easter Tuesday win at Northampton.

Early in 1947/48, he suffered a serious ligament injury in a 2-1 win over Swansea, but he was back the following season, settling into a deep-lying inside forward role and playing in that famous FA Cup win at Fulham when Johnny Devlin got the winner in extra time.

Arthur Turner then signed him for Crewe Alexandra and after he had scored 14 goals in 44 games for the Railwaymen, he moved to Stoke, who were then in the First Division. In just over a season, he got 5 goals in 23 games for them.

Albert was by then in his thirties, but the best was yet to come as he moved to Port Vale in part-exchange for Alan Martin. Arguably, Vale got the better of the bargain, as Albert went on to play in every game for Vale in that remarkable 1953/54 season, when they topped the Third Division (North). Port Vale also reached the semi-final of the FA Cup that year, losing by just two goals to one to West Brom at Villa Park.

Torn muscles ended Albert's time at Vale Park in 1956, but he played for a time for Northwich Victoria after that and then gave good service to Wednesbury Tube, the firm where he was working, in the Wolverhampton Works League. He was still doing what he did best, fetching and carrying in midfield. Albert died in 1984, but he is still remembered as a brave man who worked hard at his game and gave pleasure to the sort of fans who really know their football.

Albert 'Nutty' Newman
Midfielder, 1945-1950

	First Team Appearances	Goals
Football League	135	2
FA Cup	14	0
TOTAL	149	2

The third member of what many consider to be the greatest Walsall half-back line ever (Crutchley, Foulkes and Newman were as familiar as fish and chips to Walsall fans of the 1940s), 'Nutty' was one of many players of his era to lose virtually half their careers to the war.

Born in Lichfield in 1915, 'Nutty' was a West Brom reserve and also played for Brierley Hill before the war, and linked up with Walsall in the early days of the conflict. RAF service followed, and he was unable to play for the Saddlers until November 1945, when he played in a 2-1 defeat at Norwich. He also had a couple of games at the heart of the defence a week or two later, but in each of those (at Port Vale and Ipswich) five goals were conceded. He returned to the left side of midfield and played in all 18 games in the Third Division (South) Cup competition in which Walsall lost to Bournemouth in the final.

Then, in the first season of divisional football after the war, 'Nutty' played in every game, including the memorable 5-2 FA Cup defeat by Liverpool and the 3-0 win over Bristol City shortly afterwards, in which he opened the scoring with his first-ever goal. He missed only one game in 1947/48, when Jack Robinson, later to become assistant secretary of Wolves, deputized.

He got another of his rare goals in a 2-0 win at Port Vale in November 1948, but the following season, as he approached the age of thirty-five, he played less regularly, with both Ron Russon and Billy Green competing for his place. He stayed with Walsall for another three years as coach and then went into the building trade full-time. He had already shown his prowess during his playing career by helping with 'running repairs' at Fellows Park during the summer months.

'Nutty' was also something of a statistician, keeping fascinating scrapbooks of his career at his Brownhills home, where sadly he died in 1981. It is one of those sad coincidences that of the Walsall team just after the war, Jackie Lewis, Albert Mullard, Ron Crutchley and 'Nutty' Newman all died in their mid-sixties.

Those who saw him play will always remember 'Nutty', for (as his nickname suggested) his fine headwork, his sorties down the left flank – particularly towards the Laundry End – and his accurate free-kicks towards the far post.

Charlie Ntamark
Utility, 1990-1997

	First Team Appearances	Goals
Football League	276	12
FA Cup	23	0
FL Cup	18	1
Others	19	1
TOTAL	336	14

Charlie Ntamark was signed by Kenny Hibbitt after the manager had made a bold bid to sign Cameroon World Cup star Roger Milla in 1990. Kenny had just taken over, the club had moved to Bescot and talent was rather thin on the ground. No one, however, ever regretted that Charlie came to Walsall, as he added no small measure of skill, and saw the club through from lean times to better times.

Born in Paddington, London, Charlie played for Canon Waounde in Cameroon before linking up with Boreham Wood in this country. He had already won the first of his 31 caps for Cameroon by the time he was signed in the summer of 1990, and he played in the first League game at Bescot, wearing the number seven shirt in the opening game against Torquay. The crowd soon got behind him, appreciating his ball skills and wholehearted efforts, and his role at this time was as a midfield operator who snapped up the occasional goal. He scored twice in the space of a fortnight against Northampton and Aldershot near the end of his first season, and then in January 1992 he got a memorable match-winner at Birmingham in the Autoglass Trophy.

He retained a remarkable consistency over the years, rarely missing a game, although it was unfortunate that he had to serve two suspensions for sendings-off which seemed grossly unfair. One of these was for handling the ball when a fierce shot struck him as he stood on the line, and the other was for an alleged foul tackle at a time when, if anything, Charlie showed too little aggression. As someone trained in the legal profession, Charlie tried without success to get these wrongs righted.

He continued to give of his best throughout the 1994/95 promotion campaign, getting his first goal for nearly a season-and-a-half in the 3-1 win at Mansfield. He made a natural transition to Division Two in 1995/96. His versatility was invaluable to the side when, after the injury to Wayne Evans in the game at Bristol City in October, he took over the right-flank defence spot and held onto it even when Wayne came back four months later.

He played his 300th game at Wrexham in September 1996, but that unlucky aspect of Charlie's make-up surfaced again when a simple error on his part gave the home side the winner. He was unlucky again to be playing in that infamous FA Cup tie at Burnley two months later when the lights mysteriously went out as Walsall were leading 1-0. Perhaps unluckiest of all, he was released at the end of that season after missing only 8 of the club's 53 League and cup games.

He left behind many memories when moving to Hednesford in 1997, but neither there nor at Bromsgrove a season later did Charlie reproduce the form that he was capable of at his peak. On his day he was a class act, and one feels that with more luck he could have made an even greater impact on the game.

Martyn O'Connor
Midfielder, 1993-1996

	First Team Appearances	Goals
Football League	104	12
FA Cup	10	2
FL Cup	6	2
Others	5	2
TOTAL	125	18

Martyn O'Connor was one of several players who, over the years, have been born in Walsall and yet have come to their hometown club only after experience with other League clubs.

Born in Walsall in 1967, he played for Bromsgrove Rovers before moving to Crystal Palace in 1992. Despite coming into League football rather late, he played only 4 games for Palace. Even before he made his debut for them in November 1993 at Barnsley, he had been loaned to Walsall in the last two months of 1992/93, making his debut in a 1-1 draw against Shrewsbury and getting the match-winner at Darlington ten days later.

He played 10 games in all in that loan spell, and fans were chanting for him to be signed up, but things are never quite that simple. It was February 1994 before he came back to Bescot on a more permanent basis, the reported fee of £40,000 seeming to be money well spent. By the end of that season, he had proved his accuracy from the penalty spot, with successful conversions in successive games against Chester and Darlington. As he touched top form in 1994/95, 5 of his 12 goals were penalties, and he was voted by fellow professionals as a member of the Division Three select team. To put the lid on it all, Walsall won promotion. Martyn went on to have another excellent season in Division Two, with another 12 goals, 3 of them from the spot. He was again voted a member of the Division Two select team. It was only a matter of time before he moved on, but the move was a surprise when it came, as he went to Peterborough in the summer of 1996 for a reported £350,000.

It was something of an anti-climax that he did not settle at London Road, and after just 24 games, 3 goals and 2 missed penalties, he moved to Birmingham. It was no comfort to Walsall fans that the fee this time was £500,000.

Since then, he has graduated to captain Birmingham – just as he did Walsall – and, despite a few injury problems, he has maintained a high standard of enthusiasm and skill in midfield as the Blues have continually just missed out on promotion to the Premier League.

Martyn O'Connor had a comparatively short spell with Walsall but, like Don Dorman forty years earlier, he was an excellent captain and goal-scoring midfielder.

Richard O'Kelly

Midfielder/striker, 1980-1985 and 1988

	First Team Appearances	Goals
Football League	217	57
FA Cup	11	2
FL Cup	16	4
Others	10	2
TOTAL	254	65

Richard O'Kelly was a class performer, whether in midfield or attack, and was a deep thinker about the game – a quality which stood him in good stead in subsequent years as a coach.

Born in West Bromwich in 1957, he came to Walsall from Alvechurch in October 1979, two years after Ron Green had made the same move and four years before David Kelly followed suit. Walsall were just recovering from being relegated to the Fourth Division a few months earlier, but Richard had to wait until after their 1979/80 promotion campaign before winning a first-team place.

He made his debut in the first game of 1980/81 at Reading, playing behind front-runners Alan Buckley and Don Penn, and this role lasted throughout that season as he snapped up 7 goals himself. Like the team, he had a mixed season in 1981/82, enjoying one golden patch with a hat-trick against Newport and two goals at Gillingham in the space of a month while playing up front with Don Penn. However, he struggled in the latter part of the season, when he was in and out of the team.

He came good again in the next couple of seasons, however, getting a total of 15 goals in 1983/84 and providing the cross which Phil Neal turned into his own net at Anfield to help Walsall towards a 2-2 draw in the first leg of the Milk Cup semi-final. Later in the season, he showed versatility by playing two games on the right flank of the defence when Brian Caswell was injured.

He was leading scorer with 18 goals in 1984/85, playing up front with Steve Elliott most of the time, and then in 1985/86 he frequently played behind Steve Elliott and Nicky Cross, but still managed to score 8 goals. It was in the following summer that he moved to Port Vale. He suffered a knee ligament injury soon after making a bright start to his Vale career, but he returned after an operation and had totalled 8 goals in 37 games when Walsall snapped him up again on a free transfer in January 1988 to boost the squad as Tommy Coakley made a last push for promotion. Richard played regularly, either in the starting line-up or as sub, scored in the 4-2 win against Brentford and then deputized in defence for Andy Dornan in three of the play-off games.

At this point he moved to Grimsby, where his former Walsall boss Alan Buckley was in charge. He enjoyed a useful run, with 10 goals in 49 games as he formed an effective striking duo with Keith Alexander, but Richard then had the cruel luck to break a leg after scoring in a late-season game against Doncaster and he did not play again. He spent 1990/91 back at Port Vale as a community officer.

He rejoined Alan Buckley at Grimsby in 1991 as youth-team coach, and followed Alan to West Brom in 1995. There he remained until parting company in 2001, after working for one season with Gary Megson.

Polished, versatile, consistent and a cool finisher and a useful penalty-taker – that was Richard O'Kelly.

Granville Palin

Defender, 1960-1964

	First Team Appearances	Goals
Football League	130	10
FA Cup	3	0
FL Cup	7	0
TOTAL	140	10

Granville Palin was one of many players to give good service to Walsall after serving his apprenticeship with Wolves, and he helped to brighten up a roller-coaster spell in the early 1960s when Walsall gained and then lost a place in the Second Division.

Born in Doncaster in 1940, he was on the books of his hometown club before moving to Wolves in 1957 and playing in that unforgettable Youth Cup final in which they came back from a 5-1 deficit to beat Chelsea (who fielded the young Jimmy Greaves) 7-6 on aggregate. He had the bad luck to break a leg a year later and was allowed to move to Walsall in the summer of 1960, just after they had won promotion to the Third Division. He made his League debut against Shrewsbury Town early in October, playing on that occasion in Albert McPherson's normal position at the heart of the defence, but soon afterwards he took over at right-back to fill the place vacated by skipper Harry Haddington, who had unfortunately broken his leg.

Granville was a steady, consistent defender, but was always ready to have a go up front, and he gave a lively display in Walsall's first-ever League Cup tie at Everton in October 1960. Just over a year later he was tried there again and got one of the goals in a 5-0 win over Norwich on the day that Alan Boswell made an impressive debut in goal.

Granville became the regular penalty taker in 1962/63, and then in that sad, last game of the season against Charlton, he went in goal after Alan Boswell had been injured. Despite his best efforts, he could not prevent the visitors from winning 2-1 and sending Walsall into the Third Division.

In 1964/65, Granville had a spell in midfield, his powerful shooting from long range being a feature of his game. There were regrets from fans when he was released in the following summer. He went on to have a short spell at Worcester and then had several seasons as player-manager of Hednesford, where he played alongside former Walsall junior and future much-travelled player and manager, Brian Horton.

Granville was also a useful cricketer, playing as an all-rounder for both Walsall and Blakenall. His son, Leigh, later played for a number of Football League clubs, including Shrewsbury, Bradford City, Stoke and Hull in the 1980s and 1990s.

Granville Palin was a brave, versatile and wholehearted player. His bravery was never shown better than in the game against Chelsea in November 1961. During the match, he went back on again with a badly-bruised shin and fired in some powerful shots from midfield, as Walsall outplayed the opposition after going 5-1 down by half-time, but failed to turn the game around.

	First Team Appearances	Goals
Football League	52	0
FA Cup	7	0
FL Cup	1	0
TOTAL	60	0

Phil Parkes ranks alongside Bert Williams as the two finest of Walsall's many outstanding goalkeepers over the years. Both showed their outstanding talents while at Fellows Park and went on to give great service to First Division clubs and to play for England.

Born in Sedgley in 1950, Phil came to Walsall as a young teenager from Brierley Hill Reserves, and he was initially not retained, but then came back to sign professionally in January 1968. It was over a year later that he broke through to make his first-team debut, but he was still only eighteen when he took over from Bob Wesson for a game against Mansfield on 1 April 1969. It was no April Fool's joke, as Phil played confidently from the start – Walsall won 3-1 and he kept his place until moving to QPR for a reported £15,000 in June 1970.

Although Walsall were mid-table in the Third Division at the time, he looked a class act, and amongst some unforgettable displays was one at Fulham in a second replay of an FA Cup tie against Brighton. Thanks to Phil the game ended 0-0, and Walsall won the second replay. That £15,000 fee looked paltry as Phil missed only 5 games in his first seven seasons with Rangers. In addition, he helped them not only to promotion from the Second Division, but also to a runners-up spot in the top flight, while

himself gaining 6 England under-23 caps and a full cap in a goal-less draw against Portugal in Lisbon in April 1974.

Phil was unlucky that the remarkable consistency of Peter Shilton and Ray Clemence prevented him from gaining further England honours. After 406 games for Rangers he moved to West Ham for a reported £565,000 in February 1979. He was in the Hammers' 1980 FA Cup-winning team and in 1980/81 he kept a remarkable 22 clean sheets. He was in his fortieth year when he made the last of his 436 appearances for the Hammers, and it is one of those statistical quirks that he made exactly 344 League appearances for both QPR and West Ham.

Even after that he played three times for Ipswich Town in 1990/91 having joined them as goalkeeping coach – the last of them at Brighton in May 1991, three months short of his forty-first birthday.

Phil was originally training to be a carpenter. Few 'keepers before or since have been more effective in erecting a barrier to opponents as his 6ft 4in frame. Walsall fans were privileged to savour his remarkable

Phil Parkes (fourth from left, middle row) in the Walsall squad for the 1968/69 season, which included three goalkeepers.

anticipation, safe hands and tremendous reach in the early stages of his career. They were just unhappy tht he did not stay longer and that the fee for his transfer did not have a few more noughts at the end of it.

Phil shares with Bert Williams the distinction of being a Walsall home-grown goalkeeper who went on to play for England.

It was a remarkable coincidence that his career coincided with that of another goalkeeper named Phil Parkes. The other Parkes was no relation but was also born in the West Midlands just after the war, also stood well over 6ft tall and went on to play 382 games for Wolves.

Don Penn

Striker, 1978-1983

	First Team Appearances	Goals
Football League	141	54
FA Cup	12	2
FL Cup	6	2
TOTAL	159	58

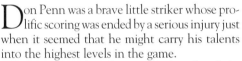

Don Penn was a brave little striker whose prolific scoring was ended by a serious injury just when it seemed that he might carry his talents into the highest levels in the game.

Born in Smethwick in 1960, he played for Newton Albion and Warley Borough before that ace star-spotter of the time, Ron Jukes, brought him to Fellows Park in 1977. Don signed as a professional in January 1978 and made his first-team debut when going on as substitute in a 1-0 defeat at Preston in April 1978. He played a handful of games in the 1978/79 relegation season, scoring against Tranmere, Lincoln and Chester, while playing up front alongside Terry Austin.

Terry moved on to Mansfield before the end of that season, and by the start of the following season Alan Buckley had returned from Birmingham. With Roy McDonough also into his stride by then there were plenty of forward options as Walsall set about going straight back up again. That they did so was mainly thanks to the fact that Don had one of those seasons strikers dream about.

He scored in the opening day win against Stockport, got two more in the first away game at Northampton, and in an unbeaten run of the first thirteen games scored eight times to bring promotion into focus. He missed only one game all season, got 26 goals while Alan Buckley got 18 and Walsall went up to the old Third Division. Could he do it again there? He opened the scoring in the first home games in both League Cup and League, but the ball didn't quite run for him as before, hard though he tried, as he was playing mainly on the right flank of the attack.

Don's greatest moment did, however, come right at the end of that season. Needing to beat Sheffield United in the final game at Bramall Lane in order to stay up, Walsall were awarded a penalty a few minutes from the end when Alan Buckley was brought crashing down. Alan was the normal penalty taker but was severely shaken by the foul on him. Don grabbed the ball and coolly beat home goalkeeper Steve Conroy from the spot. Ron Green saved a penalty at the other end before the close and Walsall stayed up.

Fittingly, Don had been featured as 'Star Visitor' in the match programme that day, and he often looked star quality again the following season, when he topscored with 15 goals (Alan Buckley was the next highest with 7) to keep Walsall up again. Liverpool were said to be interested in him, but sadly a serious knee injury kept him out for most of 1982/83. He bravely tried to play on, and actually scored against Plymouth and Bradford City in what proved to be his last two games for Walsall.

Don later played for Harrisons FC. During his time in charge of Wolves, Tommy Docherty had ambitions of bringing him back to League football, but Don's speed and finishing power had been limited by his injury and he was out of the game by his mid-twenties. Nothing dulls the memory, however, of this brave little striker shooting Walsall to victory in the few seasons he spent with them.

David Preece
Midfielder, 1980-1984

	First Team Appearances	Goals
Football League	111	5
FA Cup	6	1
FL Cup	17	5
Others	1	0
TOTAL	135	11

Walsall have had some excellent little midfielders over the years, none better that David 'Mini' Preece, who played in some of the most memorable games in the club's history and then went on to give outstanding service to Luton for over ten years and to exude class for all the teams that he played in.

Born in Bridgnorth in 1963, he was yet another discovery of former Walsall chief scout Ron Jukes. After a two-year apprenticeship, he signed professionally in the summer of 1980. He stepped out for his debut when going on as substitute for Mark Rees in a 2-1 win over Chester in January 1981 and after a few games in the following season became a vital part of the Walsall 'engine room' in 1982/83. Although it didn't ultimately win the tie, his first goal (a powerful ground shot in the League Cup tie at Preston in November 1982) was a memorable one. It was his seeming ability to cover every inch of the field with the ball and yet be in the right place to receive it that made him such an outstanding player.

His greatest Walsall days were undoubtedly in that 1983/84 run to the Milk Cup semi-final, when game after game he kept Walsall moving forward and even found time to score himself against Barnsley and Shrewsbury. He also looked the part when playing against the mighty men of Liverpool in the semi-final, particularly in the first leg at Anfield.

It was inevitable that David would be sought after by other clubs and Luton were the lucky team to get him when he moved to them in December 1984, with Steve Elliott, a useful striker, moving the other way in part-exchange. The Hatters were then in the First Division and David was a key figure as they finished in the top half of the table in three successive seasons. They also beat Arsenal in the Littlewoods Cup final of 1988, and lost to Nottingham Forest in the final of the same competition a year later.

Although they were relegated in 1992, David stayed with them until 1995, playing 394 games and scoring 27 goals. He then had short spells with Derby and on loan to Birmingham and Swindon, before joining Cambridge in the summer of 1996. He had the cruel luck to fracture a leg in his debut game against Torquay, but he was back in action again a few months later and was appointed player-coach. Although only playing occasionally at the beginning of the twenty-first century, he still set a splendid example in ball-winning, ball control and accurate passing. These are the qualities he showed throughout his long career and are the hallmark of the great midfielder. In another era he might have won more honours than the 3 England 'B' caps that he got in his Luton days.

In the summer of 2001, he followed Roy McFarland to Torquay, where he took over as assistant manager.

Andy Rammell
Striker, 1998-2000

	First Team Appearances	Goals
Football League	69	23
FA Cup	4	0
FL Cup	3	1
Others	5	1
TOTAL	81	25

Andy Rammell may have played right at the end of the twentieth century, but he was the personification of the old-fashioned striker and a mark of the impact he made with Walsall fans was that they chanted his name when he appeared on the opposite side when playing for Wycombe.

Born in Nuneaton in 1967, Andy played some of his best football in the Midlands, for it was while playing for Atherstone that he was spotted and signed by Manchester United in 1989. He didn't break through at Old Trafford, however, and moved to Barnsley in 1990. He scored 12 goals in his first season at Oakwell, to end up equal top-scorer with former Walsall striker Andy Saville. He went on to score 50 goals in 220 games before moving to Southend in 1996. Soon he was scoring against his former club, Barnsley. He came back well from a cartilage operation, but could not hold on to a regular place and on occasion showed his versatility by playing as a central defender.

He got 14 goals in 79 games for Southend, but Ray Graydon sensed that there was still some good football left in a player who was already thirty-one when he moved on a free tranfer to Bescot in the summer of 1998. How right he was, for Andy netted in five games in succession early in the season and his positive front-running was a major factor in Walsall getting into the promotion race right from the start of the season.

He sustained his efforts throughout, and his 20 goals in the season was his best tally in ten campaigns of League football and deservedly helped to take Walsall into Division One on the crest of a wave.

For a time, in 1999/2000, it seemed that Andy might score the goals to keep them there. His goals in the local derbies against Wolves, Birmingham and West Brom set the crowd roaring, but then came a niggling injury and when he came back he had to struggle for a place. Even so, he was back again near the end of the season and when he got another match-winner against Albion it seemed Walsall might just stay up.

With the arrival of new strikers for the 2000/01 campaign, Andy was transferred to Wycome Wanderers and scored twice against Walsall in October 2000, showing the finishing power and temperament for the big occasion that had characterized his time at Walsall.

Tim Rawlings
Midfielder, 1956-1963

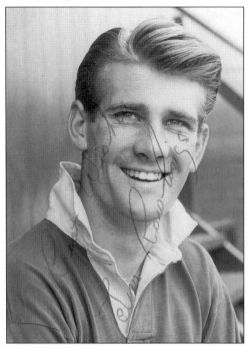

	First Team Appearances	Goals
Football League	200	5
FA Cup	6	0
FL Cup	1	0
TOTAL	207	5

Although christened Charles John, this powerful midfielder (born in Birmingham in 1932) was known as Tim throughout his career. He began with Erdington Athletic before West Brom signed him, first of all as a ground-staff boy and then as a professional in 1950. Albion had some outstanding midfielders at that time, notably Jimmy Dudley and Ray Barlow, with Billy Brookes and Gerry Summers up and coming and in quest of first-team football Tim moved to Walsall in the summer of 1956, when already nearly twenty-four. It is interesting that both Dudley and Summers followed him to Walsall a few years later.

Tim's first-team debut was in a 2-1 defeat at Gillingham at the beginning of September, but soon he was sharing in an unbeaten run of eleven games in which they scored 34 goals and made it clear that, after five successive seasons in the bottom five in the Third Division (South), better times were on the way.

Tim made the number six shirt his own, his game varying according to the opposition as he pushed forward in support of the attack when the going was good, and at other times played in a central defensive role alongside Albert McPherson when Walsall were under pressure. He was a key figure in the Fourth Division championship team, but with the arrival of Jimmy Dudley from Albion and the progress through the ranks of the young Ken Hill, Tim lost his place a third of the way through the Division Three promotion season of 1960/61. He came back into the side briefly at the end of 1961/62, and scored in the last game of the season while playing in a forward role against Scunthorpe. The following season, he played fairly regularly as Walsall battled against relegation.

No one tried harder than Tim, whether in midfield or as an emergency striker and if one powerful first-half shot in that fateful last game against Charlton had not narrowly missed the target, Walsall might well have stayed up.

It seemed too cruel that Tim was released in the summer of 1963 after battling his heart out in those last few games. He moved to Port Vale and played a few games alongside former Walsall colleague, Tony Richards.

In two seasons, Tim played 36 games for Vale and scored 2 goals, and then had spells with Nuneaton and Coleshill while working for Lucas Industries. It was perhaps appropriate that he should work for a firm that produced the means of light and energy, for in his days with Walsall he brightened up many a day with his energetic displays for the club.

Mark Rees

Winger/defender, 1979-1990

	First Team Appearances	Goals
Football League	237	37
FA Cup	12	0
FL Cup	18	5
Others	8	3
TOTAL	275	45

Mark Rees was one of the fastest wingers ever to play for Walsall and has a place indelibly written in their history for the night he ran at the Liverpool defence at Anfield and came so close to earning Walsall a sensational victory.

Born in Smethwick in 1961, Mark was yet another Ron Jukes discovery, making his League debut when going on as substitute for Jimmy Kelly in a 2-1 win over Chester in March 1979. This was an unfortunate time to be breaking through into the first team, as Walsall did not win any of their 12 remaining games that season and slipped into the Fourth Division.

Mark had still been an apprentice during his opening games, but after signing professionally during the summer he steadily eased his way into the side that won back their Third Division place just a year after losing it. At that stage, Mark was wearing the number twelve shirt as often as the number seven, and it was after going on as substitute that he got his first League goal to seal a 5-1 win over Northampton in January 1980.

In the next few seasons, he played mainly down the right flank, but also a few games as a central striker. Wherever he played, his blistering speed, genuine aggression and powerful shooting unsettled many a defence, although Mark's exuberance did get him into trouble with a few referees who could not distinguish enthusiasm from evil intent. Mark's finest seasons were undoubtedly in the mid-1980s, in both of which he reached double

figures in the goalscoring stakes, five of his goals coming in that unforgettable Milk Cup run in 1984 when he got the opener in the 2-1 win at Highbury, two more goals at Rotherham and then played a major role in the semi-final first-leg draw at Liverpool. How unfortunate it was that Mark was injured four days later in the 4-0 win over Southend, and though he bravely played in the second leg he was not able to turn on that blistering pace. That speed was in evidence again, however, in February 1985, when he got a Freight Rover hat-trick against Derby on a snow-covered pitch.

Although he suffered several more injuries, Mark completed ten seasons at Fellows Park, in the last two of which he gave some useful displays on the right flank of the defence, and that was the position in which he played in his benefit game against Wolves in May 1989.

Mark finally moved on in 1990. He had had a short loan spell with Rochdale in 1986 and subsequent clubs included teams in Ireland and France, Aldershot, Dover, Solihull and Oldbury.

He has proved himself a popular visitor to former player reunions at Bescot, as fans and former team-mates have recalled the games that he enlivened, often after coming on as substitute, and in fact his 58 substitute appearances stands as a Walsall record. There were few finer sights than Mark in full cry for goal.

Tony Richards

Striker, 1954-1963

	First Team Appearances	Goals
Football League	338	185
FA Cup	17	12
FL Cup	3	1
TOTAL	358	198

Tony Richards was voted the greatest-ever Walsall player by fans in a ballot in the late 1990s. When it comes to sorting out who was Walsall's greatest-ever goal-getter, there is little to choose between Gilbert Alsop of the 1930s, Tony Richards of the 1950s and early '60s, Colin Taylor of the 1960s and '70s, and Alan Buckley of the 1970s and early '80s.

Certainly, Tony Richards has strong claims, as he came out of the blue at a time when Walsall were struggling to survive after three successive re-election applications. Amazingly, he had been released by Birmingham City a few years earlier, and had been turned down by both Spurs and Wolves when he had trials with them after completing his National Service. Born in Smethwick in 1934, Tony stood at the crossroads twenty years later. He decided to write to Major Buckley, then manager of Walsall, for a trial and the rest is history.

He showed up so well in a reserve game that the old Major put him into the first team for a game against Bristol City in September 1954. That game was lost, but two days later Tony got one of the goals in a 2-0 win at Brentford as Walsall chalked up their first victory in thir-teen games so far that season.

He went from strength to strength from that moment on. Before Christmas he had netted a hat-trick against Reading and his two goals at Wrexham in the FA Cup earned a money-spinning third round tie at Stamford Bridge, where over 40,000 warmed to Walsall's stout-hearted efforts as they went down 2-0. By the end of the season, Tony's tally was 26 goals and he kept on scoring in succeeding seasons.

Well-placed shots, perfectly-placed headers and calm finishing touches when put through were his trademarks, and he got 10 or more goals in each of eight successive seasons. As a stronger team was built around him, he improved further still , and his best seasons were the two promotion campaigns followed by the Second Division survival season in 1961/62 – when his tallies were 26, 36 and 20 goals respectively.

1962/63 was a sad season for Walsall in many ways, not least in that Tony Richards (who had scored 8 goals thus far) was dropped after missing a penalty against Derby in March. Within a few days he had moved to Port Vale and he actually ended that season as their top-scorer, with 13 goals in 14 games. A season later, he got another 13 despite injury prob-lems, and after that Tony had spells with Nuneaton and Dudley.

Tony Richards (extreme left, second row) in the Walsall 1958/59 Fourth Division championship team.

Tony Richards was still attending games at Bescot early in the twenty-first century, the fans sitting next to him being proud to talk to a superb finisher and perfect gentleman, both on and off the field.

No other Walsall player over the years has had Tony's experience of being a member of a Walsall team that had to apply for re-election, and then a member of two other Walsall teams that secured promotion. He played alongside many striking partners, but probably the most successful combination was with former Nottingham Forest forward, Tommy Wilson.

Many fans of that era consider that the injury suffered by Tommy Wilson midway through the 1961/62 season was a key factor in Walsall's relegation a season later, for it robbed Tony Richards of the service of the through-balls that he exploited so well.

Stuart Rimmer

Striker, 1998-1991

	First Team Appearances	Goals
Football League	88	31
FA Cup	5	2
FL Cup	6	4
Others	7	7
TOTAL	106	44

Stuart Rimmer was a brave little striker who scored freely for Walsall at a time when they were sliding from the Second Division to the Fourth Division in successive seasons and when there was limited support for him up front.

Born in Southport in 1964, Stuart served his apprenticeship with Everton, and was capped by England at youth level. He played three first-team games against Swansea, Leeds, and Coventry in the old First Division, and had a loan spell to New Zealand club Hamilton before linking up with Chester in January 1985. He immediately repaid some of the £10,000 fee by getting a hat-trick in his debut game against Southend. Chester were then in the Fourth Division, and in the following season Stuart got 21 goals in the first 23 games before suffering badly-torn knee ligaments in a collision with goalkeeper Peter Wells while scoring against Orient.

This goalscoring burst had set his side on the way to promotion and Stuart was happily back early in the following season to score 14 and 28 goals respectively in the next two seasons as Chester consolidated their Third Division place. In March 1988, he moved to Watford for a reported £205,000, having scored 76 goals in 139 games, including four in a game at Preston just before his twenty-first birthday.

At Watford he played just 11 games and scored once before moving to Notts County (2 goals in 9 games) and then on to Walsall at a reduced fee – reported as being £150,000) – in January 1989 as they were tumbling out of the Second Division. He missed a penalty on his debut in a 7-0 home defeat by Chelsea in February 1989, but then got a hat-trick at Sunderland a week later to give Walsall their first win in 23 League and cup games.

His 8 goals by the end of that season were not enough to keep Walsall up, but the fans loved the all-action style of this diminutive striker. He got 18 goals in the following season (including a Leyland Daf hat-trick against Southend) but Walsall went down again, this time to the basement of the Football League. Stuart shared with Chris Marsh and Ron Green the distinction of playing in the last game at Fellows Park and the first game at Bescot, and in fact he scored Walsall's first goal at Bescot in the 2-2 draw against Torquay in August 1990.

He had got 13 goals by the following February when he moved to Barnsley for the same fee that he had cost Walsall. He got one goal in 16 games and then returned to Chester in August 1991. He had loan spells with Rochdale and Preston in 1994, and finally left the latter in 1998, having netted a club record of 134 goals in two spells.

In many ways, Stuart Rimmer was in the mould of Alan Buckley before him and Roger Boli after him – a brave little striker who showed tremendous opportunism.

Dave Serella

Central defender, 1974-1982

	First Team Appearances	Goals
Football League	267	12
FA Cup	20	0
FL Cup	17	1
TOTAL	304	13

Dave Serella was one of a number of players who gave Walsall good service after moving from Nottingham Forest in the 1970s and '80s.

Born in Kings Lynn in 1952, he was a fine all-round sportsman in his school days but he chose soccer as his main interest. When both Norwich and Nottingham Forest sought his signature, he chose Forest and he graduated via an apprenticeship to sign professionally in 1970 and to make his first-team debut in a 4-0 win over Coventry in the First Division in March 1972.

He won a regular place in the following season and played a number of games in the same line-ups as Alan Buckley, Miah Dennehy, Doug Fraser, Neil Martin and Dennis Peacock, all of whom were destined to move in due course to Walsall. Dave had played 76 games for Forest by the time he was signed by Doug Fraser, initially on loan in November 1974, making his debut in a 4-2 defeat at Charlton.

All three games were lost during that loan spell, but when he returned more permanently early in the 1975/76 season he fared rather better, partnering first Dave Robinson and then Roger Hynd at the heart of the defence. Later, he partnered Colin Harrison and Ricky Sbragia as he experienced relegation in 1979 and promotion in 1980.

Memorable games during his time at Fellows Park included the FA Cup win over Leicester in 1978, followed by defeat at Highbury and the end-of-season win at Sheffield United's Bramall Lane in 1982 that kept Walsall in the Third Division. His final season of 1981/82 was one of his best, playing in every game and partnering Peter Hart as Walsall again fought successfully against relegation.

He moved to Blackpool in the summer of 1982. In his two seasons there, the Seasiders had to apply for re-election and then just missed out on promotion. He totalled 45 games and 4 goals before moving out of the Football League and playing for Altrincham and Chorley.

Dave Serella was a distinctive centre half: craggy and moustachioed, seemingly always in the thick of the battle – one's abiding memory is of him continuing to go up for crosses with blood speckling his shirt as he played on bravely after injury.

Craig Shakespeare
Midfielder, 1981-1988

	First Team Appearances	Goals
Football League	284	51
FA Cup	21	5
FL Cup	31	8
Others	19	2
TOTAL	355	66

Craig Shakespeare was the essence of a goalscoring midfielder, and as a hitter of a dead ball was not far behind Bill Skidmore and Colin Taylor of the 1940s and 1960s respectively. What is more, he was a home-grown player and one of the many products of the Ron Jukes talent-spotting factory.

Born in Great Barr in 1963, Craig played for both Aston Boys and Birmingham Boys and after a two-year apprenticeship signed as a professional in October 1981. A year later, in September 1982, he made his first-team debut when going on as substitute for John Teasdale in a 2-2 draw at Huddersfield. He soon scored, in the home game against Brentford, and by the end of the season he was holding down a regular place.

1983/84 was a really big season for Craig as he played in every game, scored 6 goals and was involved in that tremendous run to the Milk Cup semi-final. He got 13 goals in 1984/85 and then welcomed Tommy Coakley by netting no fewer than a remarkable 17 goals in Tommy's first season of 1986/87, including 3 penalties.

He got 10 more in the 1987/88 promotion season, including a valuable goal in the play-off semi-final at Notts County. Then, in that unhappy 1988/89 season when Walsall tumbled back out of the Second Division, Craig missed only one game and his 5 goals included a strike in one of the few outstanding performances that season – a 5-0 win over Birmingham in September.

He moved to Sheffield Wednesday in the summer of 1989 for a fee reported as £300,000, and scored once in 21 games. Before the end of his first season at Hillsborough, he moved back to the Midlands to begin a three-year spell with West Brom. He skippered them in 1991/92 and 1992/93 and thrilled their fans with his powerful free-kicks and immaculate penalties. He got 16 goals in 128 games for the Baggies and then, in 1993, rejoined his former Walsall boss, Alan Buckley, at Grimsby.

Although he had spells out with injury, he impressed in central, right and left midfield during his time at Blundell Park and also did well as an emergency defender in his last season there.

He moved to Scunthorpe in 1997, but after a few games moved on to Telford for a spell as player/assistant manager in the late 1990s.

All in all, Craig played in 634 League and cup games, scored 86 goals and was in many ways the complete midfielder.

	First Team Appearances	Goals
Football League	105	5
FA Cup	8	1
FL Cup	7	1
TOTAL	120	7

Jack Shelton was an outstanding defender who had just settled into the Walsall team when the Second World War came, and he was the player who made most wartime appearances for the Saddlers.

Born in Wollaston Stourbridge in 1912, Jack was the son of Jack Shelton senior who had played for Wolves in their 1908 FA Cup final win and the stepson of another Wolves player, Jack Needham, whom his mother married after his father's early death. Jack junior played for Chase Terrace before linking up with Wolves in 1932.

He played mainly up front in those Molineux days, and it was in fact as an inside forward that he made his first-team debut for Walsall in a 2-0 defeat at Chesterfield soon after joining them in the summer of 1934. He was in and out of the team for the next two seasons, playing either up front or in midfield, but then early in 1936/37 he moved to the right flank of the defence to occupy the position held for many years by Jack Bennett.

Jack Shelton played in 92 successive games, some of them back at inside forward when Jack Bennett returned to the defence, but he had to miss the 1938/39 season through injury. His second game back in the side was in the second wartime match against Birmingham. He went on to play in a total of 194 wartime games

for Walsall and also guested on occasion for both Wolves and West Brom. In fact, he captained his former club, Wolves, on occasion.

Jack played in the final of the Third Division (South) Cup in which Walsall lost 1-0 to Bournemouth at Stamford Bridge in May 1946, but he was then thirty-four and could not command a regular place when normal divisional football was resumed in 1946/47. He moved on to Worcester in 1947 and had two good seasons with them, together with former Walsall wartime team-mates Jack Vinall and Sam Godfrey. Jack was one of the few players with a car in those days and he was well known for giving team-mates a lift.

Later, Shelton kept a newsagent's in Wednesfield, and after that served Oxford United for some years as groundsman. Jack Shelton, with his immaculately-groomed hair, was a polished defender, respected inside and outside the game. Fans were saddened to hear of his death in 1992.

Bill Sheppard

Inside forward, 1932-1935

	First Team Appearances	Goals
Football League	71	27
FA Cup	9	2
FL Cup	2	0
TOTAL	82	29

Bill Sheppard was a Geordie who travelled the length and breadth of the country in his playing career, but was immortalized in the eyes of Walsall fans when he netted the penalty that clinched the FA Cup win over Arsenal in January 1933.

Born in Ferryhill, County Durham, in 1906, Bill was on Liverpool's books in the mid-1920s after joining them from Crook Town, but it was after joining Watford in 1927 that he broke through into League football. He could scarcely have made a better start for the Hornets, as on his debut for them he netted twice in the 3-1 win over Coventry on the opening day of the 1927/28 season. By the end of the campaign, his tally was a remarkable 25 goals.

He got 14 more in the following season, but after subsequently losing his place he moved to QPR, where he scored 4 goals in 13 games in 1930/31 and then moved to Coventry (who remembered those two goals on his debut) in the summer of 1931. He did not command a regular place at Highfield Road, but he usually did well when he played and he chalked up 7 goals in 22 games before moving to Walsall in December 1932.

He was one of four ex-Coventry players (Gilbert Alsop, Chris Ball and Freddy Lee were the others) in the side against Arsenal on 14 January 1933, and it was perhaps appropriate that Walsall actually borrowed a set of Coventry shirts to play in. This was only Bill Sheppard's third game for Walsall, but he confidently banged home the penalty that was awarded in the second half after Gilbert Alsop had been fouled by young defender Tommy Black.

Bill got 16 goals, including 3 penalties, in the following season and was surprisingly released by Bill Slade in the following summer. He moved to Chester, but after only one game for them was brought back to Fellows Park by new manager Andy Wilson in October 1934. He had scored another 7 goals in 19 games by the end of the season.

After that he played for a time for Tonbridge Wells Rangers. Christmas 1950 had a shadow cast over it for Walsall fans, when they heard that Bill had died while visiting his local in Hemel Hempstead, aged just forty-four. That penalty against Arsenal has, however, guaranteed his place in the history of Walsall FC forever.

Lee Sinnott

Defender, 1982-1983

	First Team Appearances	Goals
Football League	40	2
FA Cup	4	0
FL Cup	2	0
TOTAL	46	2

Lee Sinnott looked the part as a defender from the moment he stepped out for his first-team debut as a sixteen-year-old, and it was no surprise that Walsall held on to him for less than two seasons and he went on to a long career in the top divisions.

Born in Pelsall in 1965, Sinnott was discovered playing for Rushall Olympic. After joining Walsall in November 1981, he was the third youngest player ever to appear in the first team when he made his debut on the left flank of the defence in a 1-0 defeat at Portsmouth in March 1982. He played four games that season and then, after turning seventeen during the following summer, played several games at the heart of the defence before signing professionally in November 1982. His ability to move forward and score was shown when he netted in successive games against Bristol Rovers and Brentford in the following April.

Walsall fans were agreeably surprised when he started the following season still a Walsall player, but after just four games he moved to Watford for a reported £90,000. His last game in the Walsall colours was, oddly enough, that infamous 8-1 defeat at Bolton. He had already captained the England youth team, and within eight months of arriving at Watford, he was playing in the FA Cup final.

He moved to Bradford City during the summer of 1987, after 95 games for Watford. In four seasons for Bradford, he played 213 games before moving back to the First Division (in which he had previously played for Watford) with Crystal Palace in August 1991. By this time he had also been capped at England under-21 level. He had a good first season on the left flank of the Palace defence, but struggled a little after an injury and after a month on loan he returned to Bradford City early in 1994.

In just over a year he played another 40 games for the Valley Paraders and then moved to captain Huddersfield for a spell as they went up to Division One through the play-offs in 1995. He stayed with Huddersfield just long enough to make exactly 100 appearances for them, and then in the summer of 1997 he moved to Oldham, was loaned back to Bradford City (his third spell with them) in March 1998, and finally signed off his long League career with Oldham in 1999.

Lee Sinnott played in a total of 605 League and cup games, scored 12 goals and was the ideal defender: dominant in the air, a good tackler and user of the ball, with genuine vision. He was also something of a long-throw expert when required, and one cannot say more than that he fulfilled that exceptional early promise that caused Walsall to sign him from Rushall Olympic.

Bill Skidmore

Defender, 1945-1951

	First Team Appearances	Goals
Football League	99	10
FA Cup	8	1
TOTAL	107	11

Bill Skidmore, whose legendary left foot was still being talked of by Walsall fans fifty years after he had retired, was one of a host of young Wolves players who moved to Walsall at the end of the Second World War in quest of the first-team experience that was denied them by the wealth of talent at Molineux.

Born in Barnsley in 1925, Bill played in Brampton Ellis Senior School team alongside another future Wolves and Walsall player, Henry Walters, before linking up with Wolves' Yorkshire nursery club Wath Wanderer. He then moved south and made his debut for the wartime Wolves in a 6-2 defeat by West Bromwich, where he felt that it was an honour to be on the field alongside such well-known names as Dickie Dorsett and Dennis Westcott on the Wolves side and Sandy McNab and Len Millard in the Albion side.

He played a total of 9 wartime games for Wolves and then moved to Walsall in time to play in a 2-0 win over Mansfield in September 1945. He signed as a professional the following summer and took his place on the left flank of the defence opposite another former Wath Wanderer and Wolves man, Irvine Methley, in the third game of post-war football – a 2-0 defeat by QPR. He did not miss a game for the rest of that season and his four goals (two of them from penalties) were a welcome extra dimension to his sterling defensive work.

Fans warmed to his powerful clearances and murmured in expectation when he moved up to take a free-kick. Woe betide the opponent who got in the way of the ball after Bill had propelled it with that famous left foot.

He suffered eye problems early in the 1947/48 season, but became the first Walsall player to wear contact lenses. With typical Yorkshire grit he mastered them, at a time when they were in their infancy, and he was back in the side by the end of that season. He was in and out of the side for the next few seasons, but even in the reserves he always provided plenty of excitement with his massive clearances and power-shooting, and on occasions he led the attack.

In his last season, 1950/51, he played in one memorable game against Millwall when Walsall won 4-0, with Bill netting both a penalty and a free-kick. At that time, Walsall were often fielding two efficient penalty takers in Bill and Johnny Devlin but, as some of them resulted from Johnny being brought down heavily, Bill was often entrusted with the spot-kick while Johnny got his breath back.

After leaving Walsall in 1951, Bill had spells with Frickley Colliery and Scarborough, both in the old Midland League. Later he worked for many years at Cortonwood Colliery, alongside former Wolves and Walsall colleague, Henry Walters.

Bill's name lives alongside those of Colin Taylor and, more recently, Craig Shakespeare, as one of the most consistently powerful goal-shooters that Walsall fans have known.

Colin Taylor

Winger, 1958-1963, 1964-1968 and 1969-1973

	First Team Appearances	Goals
Football League	457	169
FA Cup	31	11
FL Cup	14	9
TOTAL	502	189

When Bill Skidmore moved from Walsall in 1951, few fans could have envisaged that within twenty years another Walsall player would have emerged to equal and possibly even surpass the velocity of Bill's power shooting. Certainly Colin projected his rockets over a longer period, as he twice left Walsall and twice returned to show that he had lost none of his power or accuracy.

Born in Stourbridge in 1940, Colin played for his hometown club before being snapped up by Walsall chief scout Ron Jukes in February 1958, along with his left-wing partner, Peter Jeavons. Peter was destined to play only a few reserve games, but Colin's career immediately took off at Fellows Park. In one of his first reserve games he netted against his former club Stourbridge and, with namesake Brian Taylor just having moved to Birmingham, Colin made his first-team debut in the first home game of the 1958/59 season, a 2-1 win over Millwall. He got his first goal a few weeks later, in a 5-0 win at Aldershot, and by the end of that season he had banged home 12 goals.

That proved to be just an aperitif, for in the next two seasons Colin got 21 and 33 goals respectively as Walsall moved up from the Fourth Division to the Second Division. One of many high spots was his hat-trick in the 3-0 win at Bournemouth in April 1961, when promotion still hung in the balance. He kept scoring in the Second Division, totalling 20 goals in 1961/62. When Walsall had goalkeeper Alan Boswell carried off to hospital in the first half and bravely tried to get the point that would have kept them up, he got the goal in the 2-1 defeat in May 1963.

It was at this point that Colin moved to Newcastle for a reported £20,000. He netted on his debut against Derby and got 7 goals in 36 games before returning to Walsall in October 1964, just after Bill Harrison had taken over as chairman. In only his fourth game back, Colin got a hat-trick in a 4-3 win over Brentford and he looked as good as ever as he consistently reached double figures season after season.

During his brief spell as manager in 1968, Dick Graham was not the most popular man in Walsall when he sold Colin to his former club, Crystal Palace, in May 1968. Palace had remembered the blistering free-kick Colin had scored against them a few weeks earlier and Taylor's 10 goals helped Palace climb into the top flight for the first time in 1969.

Colin Taylor in full cry for goal at Fellows Park, as he attacks the Hillary Street End in the early 1970s.

Happily, Colin returned to Fellows Park again early in 1969/70, and after a quiet start got two late goals to win an FA Cup third replay against Brighton just before Christmas.

Walsall played Palace in the next round, but for once Colin missed a fairly straightforward chance and the game was lost. He did, however, have a few more shots in his locker. He became Walsall's penalty king in 1970/71 and netted an unstoppable shot from the spot in the memorable 3-0 win over Aston Villa in January 1971.

Colin finally bowed out in 1973, playing his last game at Blackburn when he went on to substitute for another namesake, Brian Taylor, in January of that year. In that last season he was still thrilling reserve-team fans by continuing to give of his best, just as he had done in early reserve games fifteen years earlier. He had a short spell with Kidderminster and then concentrated on his plumbing business. At the beginning of the twenty-first century he was a popular visitor to past player reunions, his modesty belying the fact that he was rightly known as 'Cannonball' for shooting power that few players anywhere in the world have equalled.

Adrian Viveash

Central defender, 1995-2000

	First Team Appearances	Goals
Football League	202	13
FA Cup	15	2
FL Cup	12	0
Others	13	1
TOTAL	242	16

Adrian Viveash was a splendidly consistent defender during five seasons at the end of the twentieth century and, much though they admired him during his time at Walsall, many fans felt that there was a sort of poetic justice in the fact that, having left for Reading in the summer of 2000, Adrian was in the side that Walsall pipped for promotion in that unforgettable play-off final at the Millennium Stadium.

Born in Swindon in 1969, Adrian was an apprentice with his hometown club before signing professionally in 1988. In seven years there he played some useful games, but he did not hold a regular place and was loaned briefly to Reading in both 1993 and 1995, the second of these spells following a broken leg that he unluckily sustained on a pre-season tour of Cyprus in 1994.

He had a further loan spell, this time at Barnsley in August 1995. Then, in October 1995, he moved to Walsall, initially on trial. He made his debut in a 2-1 home defeat by Wrexham, but fans were soon chanting 'sign him up', as they assessed the quality of his defensive work and use of the ball. Soon after being signed more permanently, he was forming an effective central defensive partnership with Derek Mountfield, and the pair did much to consolidate the Division Two place that Walsall had won a few months earlier.

1996/97 saw him voted Player of the Season for the second time in succession, and this was the time when his ability to get on the end of set pieces brought him 5 goals in 7 games around the turn of the year and 10 in the season.

He played a major role in the 1998/99 promotion win, though Richard Green and Ian Roper put him under pressure for the central defensive places, and he missed seven games in all. Then, in the very tight battle against relegation in 1999/2000, he took over the captaincy from Neil Pointon, and kept battling away in one game against Ipswich with his head heavily bandaged. Even when there were rumours of him possibly moving at the end of the season, he gave his all for the club.

He did move to Reading in the summer of 2000, and linked up with another former Walsall player, Martin Butler, but Walsall had the last laugh, winning two and drawing one of the three games against Reading during the season. In view of his great record in his five years with Walsall, most fans gave him the benefit of the doubt when his elbow laid out Tony Barrass in the last few minutes of the play-off final. Adrian was certainly one of Walsall's best-ever free-transfer signings – a defender who could make use of the long and short ball, snatch goals and organize his defensive colleagues.

Harry Wait

Goalkeeper, 1923-1930, 1936

	First Team Appearances	Goals
Football League	264	0
FA Cup	11	0
TOTAL	275	0

Harry Wait spent virtually all his working life with Walsall Football Club, his service in one capacity or another extending over no fewer than thirty-seven years. There have been no more consistent goalkeepers over almost a ten-year period, and yet he didn't come to the club until he had reached an age when many players are thinking about retirement.

Born in Darlaston in 1892, he had played on numerous occasions for his home-town club against Walsall in the old Birmingham League before Walsall's secretary-manager, Joe Burchell, signed him in August 1923. Could he make the transition to League football at the age of thirty-one? Many were unsure, but from the moment Harry's safe hands kept a clean sheet on his debut at Rotherham on the opening day of the 1923/24 season, there was no doubt at all.

He missed only one game in that first season – and that was a suspension resulting from his over-zealous protests at a goal that was awarded to Chesterfield, when Harry claimed to the end of his long life that the ball had not crossed the line. He then went on to play for three-and-a-half seasons without missing a single League or cup game. That run of 189 successive appearances came to an end when a boil on an embarrassing part of his anatomy kept him out of an FA Cup replay at Middlesbrough in January 1929.

Harry then lost his place to up-and-coming Fred Biddlestone in the first half of 1929/30, but won it back after Fred had moved to Aston Villa. Roy John, the converted full-back, then took over later in 1930 and Harry, at thirty-nine, became the first-team trainer. He was 'on the trainer's bench' for the memorable FA Cup win over Arsenal in January 1933 but, amazingly, in 1936 an injury to Peter McSevich left Walsall with a goalkeeping crisis and Harry played another five games at the age of forty-four, conceding only one goal in each.

He then continued as trainer and during the war years looked after team affairs in the absence of a full-time manager. He did a good job too, and those old enough to remember those games will testify to the quality and excitement of the games played. Harry Hibbs moved in as manager in 1945, and in 1950 Jack Nelson took over as head trainer and Harry Wait took over as groundsman for the next two years.

Harry continued to live in Wallows Lane, opposite the ground, after his retirement and watched the Saddlers almost right up to his

Harry Wait is pictured here (fourth from left, back row) as Walsall's trainer at the time when they beat Arsenal 2-0 in a third round FA Cup tie on 14 January 1933.

death in 1975. Into his eighties, Harry had a thorough grasp of his football, and a fair amount of material in this book has been inspired by conversations with Harry in his latter days.

It was Harry who was first approached by a small fair-haired boy, who asked: 'How do I get a trial as a goalkeeper, mister?' The boy was Bert Williams, who went on to play 24 times for England. Bert never forgot his old mentor. Although he was told many times to call him Harry, Bert always referred to him respectfully as 'Mr Wait'.

Jimmy Walker

Goalkeeper, 1993-present

	First Team Appearances	Goals
Football League	276	0
FA Cup	22	0
FL Cup	19	0
Others	19	0
TOTAL	336	0

Jimmy Walker has given tremendous service to Walsall during their steady rise in the football world in the second half of the 1990s and ranks amongst their very finest free-transfer signings of all time.

Born in Sutton in Ashfield in 1973, he was a junior with Notts County before moving to Walsall in August 1993. Soon he was making his debut in a 1-0 win over Gillingham in October 1993, and although he was taken off injured in the closing stages, he was back again for the next game and he kept Mark Gayle out of the team for most of that season. He had the bad luck to break a leg in a game against Colchester near the end of that season and Jimmy had to wait exactly a year for another first-team chance, so well did Trevor Wood play in 1994/95. It was an injury to Trevor, in fact, that let Jimmy back in for the final game at Bury in the 1994/95 Division Three promotion season.

1995/96 saw Jimmy and Trevor contesting the first-team spot, Jimmy's finest hour coming in December 1995 when he played on and kept a clean sheet against Swindon, despite suffering from a shoulder injury that was to keep him out for several weeks.

Jimmy's bravery often got him injured, and he sometimes got on the wrong side of referees. Early in 1996/97, he lost his place for a few weeks after being sent off at Chesterfield and turning an ankle at Bristol City in the space of a month. 1997/98 was his best season up to then, playing in all 62 games despite suffering a nasty-looking injury at Northampton just after Christmas. He has never played better than at Old Trafford, when his skill and bravery limited Manchester United to five goals in the fourth round FA Cup tie at Old Trafford.

He was again an ever-present in the 1998/99 promotion season. He saved no fewer than six penalties in the shoot-outs that took Walsall to the final of the AutoWindscreen competition, and he was voted Player of the Season. Then, in the following campaign, his run of 157 successive League and cup games came to an end, but he kept Walsall in games that they would otherwise have lost as they struggled in vain to stay in Division One.

A major factor in them ultimately going down was the harsh sendings-off that Jimmy suffered early in the season at Nottingham Forest and late in the season at home to Barnsley. Happily, he helped Walsall back into Division One at the end of the 2000/01 season. Amongst his great feats were his penalty save in the late-season League game at Stoke, and though he did make one slip in the play-off final at Reading, he came back to be his usual inspiration to the team. He was

Jimmy Walker watches the action, poised to defend his goal.

deservedly voted Division Two goalkeeper of the year by his PFA colleagues and, to top it all, he passed Mick Kearns's previous record of appearances by a Walsall goalkeeper just before the end of the season. What a triumph for both, as Mick's coaching had been a major influence on Jimmy's goalkeeping.

Jimmy is small for a goalkeeper, but his heart is one of the biggest. Known as 'Whacker' because of the power of his clearances, he is one of the finest of many great Walsall goalkeepers over the years.

Henry Walters
Midfielder/defender, 1946-1953

	First Team Appearances	Goals
Football League	254	2
FA Cup	12	0
TOTAL	266	2

Henry Walters was another excellent product of the Wath Wanderers/Wolves production line. Born near Rotherham in 1925, he made his first wartime appearance for Wolves in August 1942, playing alongside the legendary Stan Cullis in a 2-0 defeat at Villa Park. He played 30 games for Clapton Orient (as they were then) towards the end of the war, when colliery joiners from Yorkshire were moved to London to carry out essential repairs after war damage.

It was in the summer of 1946 that Henry moved to Walsall, but first-team opportunities were limited at first, with the famous Crutchley, Foules and Newman half-back line performing so consistently. He did, however, play four games on the right side of midfield at the end of that first postwar season, three of them being won and the other drawn.

He won a regular place in 1947/48, and then in the following season he was moved into defence for an FA Cup tie at Fulham and performed splendidly as Walsall won 1-0 on the ground of a team on their way up to the First Division. In six seasons, Henry missed only 14 games, giving of his best whether in midfield or defence and being one of the comparatively few shining lights in a team that in his last two seasons had to apply for re-election.

Henry seemed to play each game with a smile on his face and he richly repaid the privilege that Walsall gave him of being able to train up north and travel to the Midlands just for games. Even with a car that he had purchased (not many players had them in those days), Henry grew weary of the 200-mile weekly round trip. Walsall allowed him to move for just £750 in the summer of 1953, and what good value Barnsley got as he played for them for seven seasons.

He played a total of 172 games for the Tykes and then moved on to manage Wombwell for six seasons. He worked at Cortonwood Colliery until his retirement in 1984, and for a time worked in his son John's motor body repair business. He also learned to play an electric organ and took immense pleasure in listening to classical composers.

Henry played in charity games until nearing the age of fifty, and his love of Walsall was underlined by the fact that he kept his old claret and blue shirt for the rest of his days. He died in 1994, and a few years later an article on his career appeared in a Walsall v. Barnsley programme. A Barnsley player showed it to one of Henry's daughters and she wrote a very pleasant letter thanking the author for his tribute to her dad. It is good to know that a great player and grand man has left behind a lovely family.

Bert Williams

Goalkeeper, 1937-1945

	First Team Appearances	Goals
Football League	25	0
FA Cup	1	0
Others	2	0
TOTAL	28	0

It was a lucky day for Walsall Football Club and for football in general when a little fair-headed boy walked into the ground and asked the trainer of that time, Harry Wait, if he could have a trial. Harry, a fine goalkeeper himself in his day, tried a few shots at the lad and immediately asked the manager of that time, former Scottish international Andy Wilson, to have a look at the lad. 'He's got a bit of idea', said Harry, in one of the biggest understatements of all time. The lad, of course, was Bert Williams, destined to win 24 England caps and to be known worldwide as 'The Big Cat'.

Born in Bradley, Bilston, in 1920, Bert had played for a time for Thompsons FC in the Wolverhampton Works League after leaving school. He was still only seventeen when he made his first-team debut in a 3-1 defeat by Bristol City in October 1937. City were to loom large in young Bert's experience, as in the return game in the following February at Fellows Park, Walsall crashed 8-2. Even so, the young Bert retained his early promise and really came into his own during the war years, when he served in the RAF but still managed to play 114 times for Walsall and played for England in a wartime international.

He moved to Wolves early in the last wartime season of 1945/46, after seeming to be about to sign for Chelsea and, ironically, his debut for Wolves was in a 1-1 draw at Chelsea in September 1945. He was the man in possession when normal divisional football was resumed in August 1946 and Bert's baptism ended in a 6-1 win over Arsenal.

He was Wolves' first choice from then until 1957, winning an FA Cup winners' medal in 1949, a League Championship medal in 1954 and gaining 24 England caps between 1949 and 1955. His full tally of games for Wolves was 420, and he later owned sports shops and a goalkeeping school. In the year 2001, he spoke movingly at the memorial service of his former Wolves boss, Stan Cullis, who had played with and against him and had also managed him.

Few goalkeepers have been more agile than Bert Williams, and few as daring. Many of his greatest games were in the Walsall goal in those wartime games, and not the least of his achievements was that he could usually dodge onrushing forwards, who sometimes landed up in the net themselves.

Bert Williams (fifth from left, second row) is pictured here as a member of the Walsall playing staff. On his right is Harry Wait, the Walsall trainer at the time, who gave him his first trial. Next to Harry is Ken Tewkesbury, the goalkeeper who competed with Bert for the first-team spot just before the war, and who was one of the first players to use contact lenses. The picture is taken in front of the Wallows Lane home stand at Fellows Park, with its distinctive claret and blue stripes – the team colours until 1949.

	First Team Appearances	Goals
Football League	74	27
FA Cup	8	4
TOTAL	82	31

There were times when Dennis Wilshaw looked like anything but a future England striker, but it was during his time with Walsall that he showed the sort of form that was to blossom at the highest level a few years later.

Born in Stoke in 1926, Dennis played for Packmoor Boys Club in the North Staffordshire League before moving to Wolves and making his debut in the 4-1 defeat at West Brom in September 1943, in a wartime game. He scored his first goal in the return fixture a week later and he had netted 5 times in 13 games by the time he was loaned to Walsall in February 1946. He scored in a 2-2 draw against Notts County on his debut, when future Wolves colleague Johnny Hancocks got the other goal.

Wilshaw had got 4 goals in 10 games by the end of that season in which Walsall reached the final of the Third Division (South) Cup, and he was a natural choice for one of the inside forward positions when normal League football was resumed in August 1946. Playing first at inside forward and then on the left wing, he netted 21 goals that season. These included one in the FA Cup tie against Liverpool when Walsall went down 5-2, and a hat-trick in the Easter Tuesday 8-0 win at Northampton.

By the end of that season, he was playing alongside Doug Lishman in one of the most successful partnerships the club has ever fielded. Both had excellent seasons in 1947/48, when Walsall finished third in the Third Division (South), Dennis getting 9 goals and Doug 21.

While Doug moved to Arsenal in the following close season, Dennis was recalled by Wolves after three more games in 1948/49. He then played regularly in Wolves' reserve team until late that season, when he got a hat-trick on his first-team debut against Newcastle. By an interesting coincidence, this was the game broadcast on BBC radio that afternoon and so Dennis got national publicity. By the end of the season he had got 10 goals in 11 games, but he missed out on a place in the FA Cup final.

Dennis went from strength to strength with Wolves, sharing in their 1953/54 League Championship win, when he got 25 goals, and playing 12 times for England, getting four goals in the 7-2 win over Scotland in April 1955. After totalling 112 goals in 119 games, he moved to Stoke in 1957. There he got 49 goals in 108 games, before his career was ended by a broken leg sustained in an FA Cup tie against

Dennis (extreme right) is pictured here in a Wolves v. Albion game at The Hawthorns in the 1950s. As the photograph indicates, Dennis had a knack of being close to the goalmouth action. Here, he watches Roy Swinbourne challenging Albion goalkeeper Norman Heath, ready to challenge for any possible loose ball. The Albion player with his back to the camera is Joe Kennedy, one of the many defenders in that era who had a healthy respect for Dennis's finishing power.

Newcastle in February 1961, nearly twelve years after his famous hat-trick against the same opposition.

Dennis later became head of the service and community department at Alsager College near Crewe. Sometimes Dennis had looked ungainly on the ball, but he had remarkable skill and finishing power, and it was one of his characteristics that he was equally effective as goal-maker and goalscorer in whatever level of the game he played.

	First Team Appearances	Goals
Football League	125	38
FA Cup	13	7
FL Cup	8	3
Others	6	1
TOTAL	152	49

Although he was thirty-three when he joined Walsall, Kevin Wilson had three excellent seasons there and maintained a high level of consistency at a time when the whole team were on the upgrade.

Born in Banbury in 1961, he played for his hometown club before moving to Derby County for a reported £20,000 in December 1979. Despite being slightly-built (that may have been why Stoke and Sheffield United had rejected him after trials), he gradually got into his goalscoring stride and he hit a purple patch soon after Arthur Cox, a former Walsall coach, was appointed manager in 1984. In the space of four days, he got four goals against Hartlepool and a hat-trick against Bolton. He had got 13 goals in 14 games that season when he broke an arm in a game against Plymouth. Soon after his recovery he moved to Ipswich, in January 1985. By that time he had totalled 41 goals in 141 games for the Rams and at Portland Road he kept up this healthy rate, netting 49 more goals in 123 games before moving on to Chelsea in 1985.

At Stamford Bridge he competed with Gordon Durie for the position as Kerry Dixon's striking partner, and though he spent some time on the substitutes' bench, he still managed to score 55 goals in 191 games.

He played a deeper role with Notts County between 1992 and 1994, getting 3 goals in 81 games and having a short spell on loan to Bradford City. It was in the summer of 1994

that he came to Walsall as player-coach, and after sharing in a 1-1 draw at Fulham on his debut, he got two of the goals in a 4-0 first leg League Cup tie against Plymouth.

His skill and determination made him everyone's favourite, and his achievement in playing in all 52 League and cup games and scoring 22 goals were integral parts of Walsall's promotion win. His dual spearhead with Kyle Lightbourne tormented Division Two defences, just as they had done those in Division Three and Kevin was again an ever-present in 1995/96, getting another 19 goals in 56 games.

And so to 1996/97, when in a rather unhappy season his run of 137 successive games came to an end when he was omitted for a game on an icy pitch at Wycombe in December and he was cruelly sent off in a game at Bury – his first dismissal in nearly twenty years in the game.

While with Walsall, Kevin took his tally of Northern Ireland caps to 42 and some fans felt that he might well have been appointed manager when Chris Nicholl left in the summer of 1997. As it was, he moved to Northampton as assistant to Ian Atkins while continuing to play occasionally, and in 1999 he became manager and scored his 199th goal in League and cup football.

Kevin Wilson has been an outstanding professional, a tremendous opportunist and an inspiration to team-mates. Whatever he achieves in the future as a manager, his years with Walsall as player-coach will never be forgotten.

Bernie Wright

Striker, 1971-72 and 1973-77

	First Team Appearances	Goals
Football League	167	40
FA Cup	19	7
FL Cup	10	1
TOTAL	196	48

Bernie Wright was everybody's dream of a powerhouse striker, able to score goals with head and feet and to create space for others in the danger area. What is more, he came to Walsall, just as Tony Richards had done nearly twenty years earlier, at a time when he needed a club just as much as Walsall needed a striker.

Born in Birmingham in 1952, he, like Tony Richards, had a spell with Birmingham City. He was then released and sought a trial with Walsall after doing well with Paget Rangers, the club another Walsall striker Doug Lishman had played for some twenty-five years earlier. Bill Moore was manager at the time and he gave Bernie a first-team chance almost immediately. Wright made his debut on 2 October 1971, when he got the second goal in a 2-0 win over Port Vale. Soon he was to score in the first three rounds of the FA Cup, putting out Dagenham, Brighton and Bournemouth to earn a fourth-round tie at Everton. Walsall lost this 2-1 but Bernie created such an impression by his challenge up front that Harry Catterick almost immediately signed him for the Toffees.

Just a month after that FA Cup tie, Bernie was stepping out as substitute for Gary Jones in a 4-0 defeat by Liverpool at Anfield. He scored an opportunistic goal to earn a point at Bramall Lane and he again hit the net against West Ham in the following season. However, he didn't command a regular place, and reported off-field problems saw him being released after just 10 games. As a result, he returned to Walsall in January 1973.

After a few games to get back his edge, Bernie scored a thrilling winner deep into injury time in the 4-3 win over Bristol Rovers in March 1973, and a few weeks later he scored in three successive games. Bernie's best season was 1974/75, when he played a major part in the FA Cup wins over Manchester United and Newcastle, totalled 10 goals in the season and played a part in many of Alan Buckley's 25 goals. Wright got 12 more goals the following season, but soon after scoring twice in a 5-1 win over Sheffield Wednesday in February 1977, he was allowed to move to Bradford City.

Manager Doug Fraser convinced chairman Ken Wheldon that he had been sold for a fair price, but fans were disappointed. Meanwhile, Bernie helped Bradford City in the last stages of their run to promotion from the Fourth Division, and got 10 goals in the following season when they went straight back down again.

A total of 13 goals in 69 games did not reflect Bernie's value in the side, nor did the 24 in 81 games that he got after joining Port Vale in the summer of 1978. He was Vale's Player of the Year in 1978/79 and after leaving them in 1980, played for Kidderminster, Trowbridge, Cheltenham, Worcester and Gloucester.

Bernie was one of the biggest and best of Walsall's strikers over the years. With his large sideburns, he was a fearsome sight to defenders when he charged through the middle. Walsall managed to sign him twice, and fans of the time just wished that they had hung on to him longer.